I.D. CRISIS

**FREEDOM OF CHOICE:
TRUE LIFE
OR
HUMAN NATURE**

I.D. CRISIS
FREEDOM OF CHOICE:
TRUE LIFE
OR
HUMAN NATURE

by Kurt Koppetsch

SHEPHERD NEWS TRUST
WEST BOYLSTON, MASSACHUSETTS 01583

Copyright © 1985 by Kurt Koppetsch

Library of Congress Cataloging in Publication Data

Koppetsch, Kurt, 1935—
I.D. CRISIS
   Freedom of Choice—True life or human nature
Includes Index
   1. Religion—Christianity.   2. Psychology—Attitudes,
Behavior.   3. Sociology—Human Trends.   I. Title.

Library of Congress Catalog No. 85-050153

ISBN 0-933663-00-5

Printed in the United States of America

To Tante

*Her life of giving and caring made God's
love real.*

Acknowledgment

Encouragement is a basic human need. The support from people around us—family, friends, sometimes even strangers—is essential to success in shaping ideals into reality. Positive inputs leave their imprints on our decisions.

I have been fortunate in my writing of I.D. CRISIS because of a generous assortment of people around me. Some conveyed their opinions more vociferously than others, only to strengthen my convictions that life is a continuous struggle and in need of constant attention.

But I have also found answers for persevering by doing what we believe is right and what is accepted by others as just. The Golden Rule prevailed in times of conflict and controversy as I have seen demonstrated that severe tests in life are blessings that refine the hidden and inner qualities of true life. For overtowering all manner of hardships were friends ready and willing to help.

But in all these experiences I also met people in need of hope. I have seen people of all walks of life struggle to cope in their specific life situations—some suffering more than others. Their needs must become our concern.

Because I do not want to miss any of my family or friends in special recognition, therefore to all I say, "Thank you for support and encouragement." A separate word of appreciation is indeed appropriate to my editor, Mr. Darrell Turner.

Biblical quotations are from the Revised Standard Version of The Bible, Copyright 1946, 1952, © 1971, 1973 by the National Council of the Churches of Christ in the United States of America, and are used by permission. Biblical quotations identified by TEV following the reference are from the Good News Bible—Old Testament: Copyright © American Bible Society 1976; New Testament: Copyright © American Bible Society 1966, 1971, 1976.

October 1985   Kurt Koppetsch

Editor's Preface

"Doing theology" was a popular expression in ecclesiastical circles in the 1960s and 70s. It was meant to illustrate the importance of the individual's determining the actions of God in his or her life. Scholars often made the point that each of us is a theologian in that we have developed our own belief system, either within the framework of Christianity or outside it.

With the rise of new social and political movements have come new forms of theology, prefaced by different adjectives. Examples include black theology, feminist theology, process theology and liberation theology. It sometimes seems as though every interest group has its own theology!

This book might be called an example of "theology in the workplace." The author draws on his experiences as an engineer, husband and father to illustrate how the Christian faith impacts our daily lives. He frequently makes the point that God speaks to us always in His Word but sometimes also in events that seem far removed from what he calls "ecclesiastical religion."

In some ways Mr. Koppetsch addresses himself to the committed Christian, in some ways to the seeker or agnostic. As the title indicates, he believes modern people are facing an identity crisis. The solution, he affirms, is "remembering the fact that we are dependent creatures of God." (page 15)

Mr. Koppetsch examines some of the things that divert us from realizing our true identity. These include philosophies, politics, economics, and even false religions.

Throughout, he stresses that the Bible and the Holy Spirit are God's guides to lead us out of the maze of confusion to the truth of God.

The book does not pretend to contain all the answers, or to be a complete guide for the Christian life. As the author says, "no writing, however eloquent, can prescribe a step-by-step procedure for this search." (page xiii) What I.D. Crisis tries to do is to offer some suggestions for avoiding pitfalls and being able to see the forest of faith through the trees of temptation and diversion that so often throw us off the path and into a swamp of confusion.

Kurt Koppetsch is not a famous theologian or a noted writer. But he has searched the Scriptures for guidance in his own life, and has some insights to share based on his own experience of God. He and I both hope that the thoughts contained in this book will be of help to you in your own pilgrimage.

Darrell Turner

Table of Contents

xi

Introduction

I.D. CRISIS was written to alert all peoples everywhere about a better way of life, God's way. The purpose of the text is to help diligent readers get started on the personal road of discovery to eternal truth and universal salvation.

No writing, however eloquent, can prescribe a step-by-step procedure for this search. People must learn to appreciate for themselves the way of truth. Such is the beginning of an everlasting relationship.

And the authority for guidance belongs to God. In human ideas, what may be totally acceptable to some is highly objectionable to others.

Even though attitudes and behavior may vary from culture to culture, the essence of life, nonetheless, is changeless. The model of the godly life has been given to the world. The message about the Kingdom of God and the will of God is clear in Christ's teaching.

Much confusion is nourished by ignorance. And evil enters in when theories are declared as facts and dogmatic pronouncements attempt to protect doctrines and traditions. This is typical when ecclesiastical organizations feel threatened and try to perpetuate themselves. But such defensive moves are not always necessarily in the interest of truth.

There is no need to speculate concerning the truth about God. The teaching of Christ is God's summary. The message given explains the Kingdom of God and the will of God. Nothing more is required for the short human pilgrimage on earth of seventy years more or less.

Christ affirmed God's expectations of faithfulness and obedience. The call to worship and service—the ancient Shema Yisrael—is confirmed for all people everywhere as a primary event in everyday life: "You shall love the Lord your God with all your heart, and with all your soul, and with all your mind." (Matthew 22:37)

No additional explanation is needed. The human race is the height of God's creation. And God has definite expectations of people.

Eternal truth is further enhanced by Christ summarizing the historic Law of Holiness and Justice. This divine command stands as the foundation of all human relationships: "You shall love your neighbor as yourself." (Matthew 22:39)

Prior to Christ's confirmation of these standards for human behavior, God's prophet Micah provided the divine reply to the age-old question as to what God requires of people. The subject again concerns holiness and justice: "He has showed you, O man, what is good; and what does the LORD require of you but to do justice, and to love kindness, and to walk humbly with your God?" (Micah 6:8)

The direction is straightforward. There are no hidden meanings.

Yet Abraham Lincoln, one of the greatest Americans, lamented about the sad condition of ecclesiastical religion. The prophet Micah's detailed summary to "walk humbly with your God" was compared by Lincoln to the workings of the institutional church.

This is how Lincoln saw the problem: "When any church will inscribe over its altar, as its sole qualification for membership, the Saviour's condensed statement of the substance of both Law and Gospel, 'Thou shalt love the Lord thy God with all thy heart, with all thy soul, and with all thy mind, and thy neighbor, as thyself' that church will I join with all my heart and all my soul."

What otherwise may appear as sarcasm on the part of non-committed people are actually cries of desperation—sometimes even calls for reform. The vacuum within an empty soul is the greatest imaginable abyss. It is as consuming as the bottomless pit.

- Where is God in times of war?
- Why all the starvation in the world?
- Why do people suffer?

These outcries are real. Death and suffering are in the world. Where is God in all this trouble? Assuredly, with the faithful believer! God is right in the center of war, starvation, and suffering to support and uphold the faithful.

Faithful believers live in the world according to divine promise. What God ordains, God also sustains. This message of hope has been given many times. But it must be repeated again and again.

God has already demonstrated His perfect record of performance. He has proven to be faithful and steadfast. Therefore, any demands for new themes in the teaching of eternal truth are mere tactics of arrogant people. With their demands they wish God's creation to march to their tune. Anyone more concerned about the ways of the world than the Kingdom of God does not have a working relationship with the Living God at heart.

Biblical writings are sufficient evidence about the concerns of a righteous God for sinful people. The Bible, indeed, is a text on relationships. It is a true God-and-people book.

But eternal truth is a matter of revelation by the Holy Spirit. The written word, indeed, is human, but its inspirational message is divine.

God inspires believers by means of divinely ordained channels. The Bible is the means by which the Holy Spirit makes known the truth about God.

Education is a continuous process of learning. But somehow people have conceived the unfortunate notion that formal education ends the learning process. Nothing is further from the truth.

A worse situation exists in religious education. It is truly sad to see children elated at having been freed from the burden of learning about God at the day of their confirmation. They have learned fast to follow the example of elders.

With the exception of some sporadic programs, no responsibility has been exercised by either teachers or adults to maintain the learning process of knowing all the truth about God.

Good behavior is a matter of faithfulness and obedience to God. The quality of our response to God is not subject to human consideration, for the will of God is the purpose of our being. Christ taught and demonstrated God's intent for people. When people live and act accordingly, they have achieved true greatness. Then they also have something to boast about—because of what God through Christ has done—and not brag about worldly achievements.

The Word of God in Jeremiah encourages our concern for the Kingdom of God. "Thus says the LORD: 'Let not the wise man glory in his wisdom, let not the mighty man glory in his might, let not the rich man glory in his riches; but let him who glories glory in this, that he understands and knows me, that I am the LORD who practice steadfast love, justice, and righteousness in the earth; for in these things I delight, says the LORD.' " (Jeremiah 9:23-24)

This introductory text has two follow-up volumes:
PRIORITIES—A Salvation Story
COMMITMENT—Because of Truth and Faith.

October 1985   Kurt Koppetsch

1

Are We Existing in an Identity Crisis?

We live by priorities.

The routine of daily life is subject to value judgments. Our decisions have far-reaching consequences on personal behavior and relationships. The quality of life on earth depends upon a successful balancing of priorities—with God and with one another.

Choosing priorities requires people to exercise their God-given freedom. Any outcome will necessarily be influenced by personal convictions and views about life. People decide to make materialistic greed or spiritual hunger their priority. Blessing or curse of life on earth depends upon a thorough appreciation of the purpose of our creation.

To help us live by the right decision requires that we become fully aware as to whose we truly are.

Therefore, in light of God's purpose for human creation, let us ask: "Do we have an identity problem?"

Because of its serious implications, this question certainly merits attention. So let us look at the problem with genuine concern and examine the quality of daily life. Let us expose all the consequences that result from spiritual neglect. Thus, we must make our review a matter of personal involvement.

As we commit ourselves to the search for truth, we seek

to find the answers to understand the secrets of life. And any truth uncovered will hopefully guide us back on the right path of faithfulness and obedience.

A potential crisis can be turned into the better way of life. Our quest for purpose and meaning on earth will also lead to a deeper appreciation of the nature of our being. A dedicated search will lead us to fundamental truth and point the way to whose we truly are.

We are God's people!

God's mark of ownership is the divine act of our creation. And on the strength of God's righteousness alone, this claim on our lives was renewed. God made it permanent through the divine act of redemption.

God acted despite the sinfulness of people. Redemption—life in union with Christ as God's anointed savior—offers all people the opportunity to live by grace in the newness of life. It further secures for the faithful and the obedient a place of restored fellowship in the presence of God. For as grace and faith combine, then all people who believe in God's plan of salvation will experience the oneness that identifies human beings as the image of God.

If our behavior in thought and deed is not in harmony with God's expectations for the purpose of our creation, then, we are in the center of an identity crisis. Our behavior—together with the fruits of our labors—is all the evidence needed to indict us.

Whenever people as individuals, families, or societies that make up a nation continuously miss the mark of realizing the life-giving relationship ordained by God, God's expectations of faithfulness and obedience have become sidetracked. When this happens, devotion as well as service to God degenerates into a purposeless ritual. People will go to church once a week solely to satisfy the ego. The absence of any genuine sign of repentance will serve as additional proof that pride and arrogance have combined forces with selfishness and greed.

Neither families nor societies benefit from the spiritual decay of their members. Satan is the only one to gain from any degeneration of the human race. Therefore, Satan will offer help to the wayward in making the final break from knowing God by severing any remaining strains of conscience. Thereafter evil can claim victory over the conflict in man.

Sheer physical existence becomes the new order of the day. Without hope, life has already been shown to be very harsh. People compete for self-esteem, increase greed to remain above average, and excel in empire building to maintain an image.

For people who live without hope, the world is nothing more than a jungle. This type of world consumes—energies and people. In it, people will fight and kill in order to survive.

Within it, people will tend to live in their own ocean of self-righteousness. Only the choking from the corrosive atmosphere of hate and greed will make them aware of spiritual blindness. Missed opportunities to overcome this way of life lead to deathbed despair in which the dying see the horizons closing in for the final curtain call.

People have created their own death trap when they make the world a place in which ruthless ambition is the order of the day. In it we will constantly see people working extra hard to outsmart and outdo their fellow men.

As people fight for supremacy, the tenderness of conscience becomes dulled in proportion to the fierceness of worldly struggles. Eventually the wayward will also become insensitive to the pain of slow spiritual death. As they compensate for this painless loss with overindulgence in the pleasures of materialistic gains, Satan waits prepared to reap the harvest in a field full of people who have lost all spiritual identity with God.

Because human beings were created to be dependent creatures of God, an identity crisis is really upon us. We simply have failed to appreciate divine truth as the message that alone can satisfy the hunger of starving souls.

What must we do?

This is not just a cry of desperation of the humanly frail and physically weak. There are moments of truth in all people—good and bad alike. These times of root awakening are opportunities to change. It can be the beginning of the better way of life.

Unfortunately, not all people will take advantage of the chance for a new beginning. We all know that the shedding of bad habits is good for us and there is even some honesty to our hidden desire for change. Yet this is seldom pursued with sufficient impetus to make a fresh beginning the new routine of daily life.

We are not alone in this tragic situation. We share this dilemma with multitudes of people around us.

Because pride makes us cry for even greater independence, we are slaves of our own pride. It makes us want to dictate the ground rules for communion and fellowship with God.

Thus, the sin of rebellion, defiance, and independence is compounded by the greater sin of pride. Even though this conflict is harsh, let us not become overwhelmed by the fierceness of our own problems. Nor must we let ourselves become intimidated by the evil around us. There is nothing in the world that can destroy what God has ordained.

At the same time let us also recognize that there are no alternate or substitute ways for God's plans for our spiritual well-being. For on the basis of God's righteousness alone, grace is the divine gift that secures salvation through Jesus Christ. Thus, the only proper reaction to God's offer of grace is to take refuge in God our Redeemer.

Life in today's world is a mixed blessing. Aimless drift and apathy is a predominant problem among the well-to-do. Hunger, disease, and death darken all signs of hope for the less fortunate. Though present in different ways, despair can touch rich and poor alike. Nonetheless, life continues to run its course because God sustains it.

This world is the proving ground for Christian faith. The faithful and obedient are given the opportunity to live the faith that we as Christians have so readily professed. Life must be shared with zealots, opportunists, the confused, and even those who reject everything, including themselves.

Yet, the presence of God is evident. For from within this unlikely bundle of people, God continues to use individuals in many ways to accomplish divine purpose.

Through his grace, God is providing ample help. Christians can draw on the power of God to let the Holy Spirit work His will through them. Thus, we do not live for ourselves but to the glory of God.

Christ's prophetic words in the Sermon on the Mount serve to identify followers and their mission: "You are the light of the world . . . Let your light so shine before men, that they may see your good works and give glory to your Father who is in heaven." (Matthew 5:14,16)

For a better understanding of "good works," let us keep in mind the story of the Good Samaritan (Luke 10:25-37). God is glorified when we recognize the other person also as a child of God and give of ourselves.

If Christians—as the body of Christ—are really concerned about their mission and work, they need not defend or be apologetic about their witness to the good news of the Gospel: Jesus Christ came, died, and was raised back to life for the forgiveness of sins—for even the worst of sinners.

To end the identity crisis, we must yield to the Holy Spirit, who alone will reveal the truth about God.

The flourishing of falsehoods—such as religious cults— during an identity crisis is alarming, but should not come as a surprise. Whenever people feel spiritually destitute, they will accept even their own manipulation for the sake of temporary relief.

But false teaching will go on. St. Paul mentioned that this will continue as long as there are people who like to promote human ideas: "For the time is coming when people will not endure sound teaching, but having itching ears they will accumulate for themselves teachers to suit their own likings, and will turn away from listening to the truth and wander into myths." (2 Timothy 4:3-4)

As people of God—our true identity through creation and redemption—we live in the world by the grace of God.

This rules out all clever manipulation by the human mind to become giants in intellect and develop our own methods of pleasing God. Restored fellowship was provided by God two thousand years ago—despite sin—as a gift of grace.

God has acted. We now must respond, faithfully and obediently, and live out God's plan of salvation.

2

Christianity, Nice People, and the Real World

Christianity provides a working relationship between God and people.

Only within this framework is Christianity of value in the affairs of daily life. Christianity represents the new covenant, whose foundation is God's grace and righteousness.

This covenant takes on substance when, by the power of God, faith moves people to share with God the opportunity of restored fellowship. Spiritual newness of life is then experienced as togetherness with Christ.

All groups of believers will be successful whenever Jesus Christ is at the center of activities. With their confession of faith, believers acknowledge God's concern for people. The public creed proclaims Jesus Christ as God's appointed Savior.

Christianity represents the new form of life where God's gift of grace is openly welcomed. At the same time, restored fellowship with God is also faithfully practiced.

As confessing Christians, we actively respond to God's offer of life. We do this by dedicating the total self to bring glory to God. Our whole being must become a demonstration that God's plan of salvation applies to all humanity.

According to God's plan, Jesus Christ is the cornerstone. On Christ we build; and together we grow in faith. The authority of Jesus Christ over our lives is ordained by God. Christ's life has been established as the model of the godly

7

life. As the living Word of God, Christ is the teacher of truth. Through the Holy Spirit, Christ lives in us as the source of revelation for the truth about God.

Christianity is not an invention of the human mind. It was by the Holy Spirit of God moving among the people of the ancient Church that Christianity's meaning was established. As a fellowship of believers, we live out the powerful interaction of a righteous God and sinful people.

The purpose of Christianity—as ordained by God—is described by Christ in terms of eternal life: "And this is eternal life, that they know thee the only true God, and Jesus Christ whom thou hast sent." (John 17:3)

The vehicle available to God for bringing this point across is then the fellowship of believers, better known as the Church of Christ.

Though God uses people in this work of witness on behalf of God's Kingdom, the propagation of truth remains definitely a matter of the Holy Spirit. This is not at all the activity of the human mind.

Human intellect is prone to manipulate truth through interpretation—even the truth of the Word of God. Therefore, God does not select people to become witnesses to the good news about the Kingdom according to cleverness and charisma. God chooses and calls believers on the basis of faith. Faithful and obedient people already have dedicated themselves for service to God. Only then can the Holy Spirit work God's will through them.

St. Peter, inspired by the Holy Spirit, defined the authority of Christ's Church and exemplified its mission: "Let all the house of Israel therefore know assuredly that God has made him both Lord and Christ, this Jesus whom you crucified . . . And there is salvation in no one else, for there is no other name under heaven given among men by which we must be saved." (Acts 2:36, 4:12)

In a historic sense, Christianity traces its roots to a specific event in time and place, as God has chosen to reveal Himself in the person of Jesus Christ.

Jesus Christ came, died, and was raised back to life for the purpose of redeeming sinners. God intervened in human creation to give all people the hope of eternal life.

But full appreciation of the Gospel demands spiritual comprehension of our total heritage. Divine truth in Old Testament and New Testament alike is God's blessing for each day. Biblical literature, like the Book of Genesis, therefore, must be read and understood in terms of the Gospel. Similar considerations apply also to the prophetic writings and the Psalms.

Our status as redeemed people is sustained by God's grace through Jesus Christ. Believers in Christ can claim this blessing because of God's righteousness. As part of God's steadfastness, grace is constantly renewing sinful people.

This universal truth is captured in Christ's answer to Peter's question whether seven times seven is a good limit to forgive those who wrong us. Christ's reply, "I do not say to you seven times, but seventy times seven" (Matthew 18:22), points to the limitless love of God. Christ now wants believers to share this truth with other people. As we forgive those who have wronged us, in like manner will God forgive us our sins.

But there are problems with this truth in the world. The act of God's grace is being tied to human performance. The merciless sarcasm of non-believers wants to indict God's chosen people as not being worthy of their calling because the fellowship of believers should consist only of "nice people."

This is nothing but an evil diversion. It dilutes all effectiveness of the grace of God. It ridicules the love of God that is constantly working the spiritual regeneration of sinful people.

As Christians, we must not feel intimidated by worldly opinions of people who are outside the fellowship of believers. Yet, it is a Christian's duty to witness to these people, even though they may reject our witness to God's truth by showing greater interest in the frailty of our human nature than for God's message in the Gospel.

The evil in humanism surfaces when specific shortcomings among Christians are singled out as the reason for rejecting God's message of the Gospel and ultimately rejecting God.

Christians live in the world to be "like light for the whole world" and not for satisfying worldly intellectual concepts or personal ambitions. Christ's teaching is clear on this subject. The charge is precisely stated that a Christian's "light so shine before men, that they may see your good works and give glory to your Father who is in heaven." (Matthew 5:16) Thus, commission for Christian witness originates from God through Christ.

Only uncommitted people, like those with a totally humanistic view of life, will want to shy away from making the necessary commitment of dedication to God. So they will select only those priorities that are to their liking.

Jesus has told us that "each tree is known by its own fruit." (Luke 6:44) This message helps in identifying true believers, for Christians are set apart—even in the jungle of life that is the real world—as children of God.

"The good man out of the good treasure of his heart produces good, and the evil man out of his evil treasure produces evil; for out of the abundance of the heart his mouth speaks." (Luke 6:45)

Out of a fellowship of a few believers has grown the largest religion in the world. This was possible because the early Church served God in the unity of the Spirit. The Apostolic Church overcame "isms" and overwhelmed religious cults because it relied on Jesus Christ as its Lord and submitted to the guidance of the Holy Spirit.

Different isms and even more sinister cults challenge Christianity now. Indeed this has been the case throughout the ages ever since the days at Antioch, for "in Antioch the disciples were for the first time called Christians." (Acts 11:26) As confessing followers we have no choice in the matter of faith.

God has ordained spiritual salvation and restored fellowship for all mankind. With it a love relationship has been established between God and people in its most perfect and simplest form.

But what had started out to be perfect and simple soon turned out to be very complicated. People started intellectualizing Christianity. Soon sophistication permeated the affairs of daily life. Concepts of "true philosophy," "correct way of life," "humanism," and more recently "fundamentalism" became like a non-functional appendix in the relationship of God and people.

The present dilemma is frightening but definitely not hopeless. God already has acted. As believers, let us therefore refresh our memory as to whose we truly are. Then let us find refuge in the divine promise that Christ is with us. This is the only way we can learn to rely on God's message of hope.

Ecclesiastical religion—acting strictly on the authority of its own doctrines and dogmas—has constantly been more eager to denounce and condemn rather than to demonstrate the truth of the Gospel. Even quite recently a theology professor from a major Christian tradition discussed the problem of fundamentalism in a way that focuses on exposure of the wrong instead of enlightening people in the

truth. (Fundamentalism: A Pastoral Concern. Fr. Eugene
LaVerdiere, S.S.S. The Liturgical Press, Collegeville,
Minnesota, 1983) But the overriding issue in Christian
witness is truth. Only truth can enlighten people.

For example, ecclesiastical theology teaches human wisdom. It makes people appear wise and pious in the eyes of
the world. But in divine wisdom God says, "Know that I am
God and have faith." Faith makes a believer act to bring
glory to God.

Faith—the human response to God's grace—has been
neglected for centuries as church doctrine placed greater
emphasis on worldly accomplishments of good works. This
and numerous other religious decrees—by the authority of
councils or boards—had as their objective the control of the
membership instead of concern for the Kingdom of God.

In other instances the church, as an ecclesiastical institution, has dictated scientific truth. And even today there are
Christian groups who insist on teaching creation according
to the Genesis account, despite best available knowledge
that the planet earth has existed for 4 1/2 billion years.

People are conditioned not to question anything declared sacred by the church. Because the general membership further assumes that its clergy have greater knowledge
about church precepts, they dare not question what is
being taught. History has shown that ecclesiastical rules
have favored the church as an institution instead of address-
ing the needs of people and their relationship to God.

Smoke screens conceal decisive issues. The world is full
of programs that water down the truth. Somehow "nice
people" do not wish to show their own true colors, as this
declaration may demand a commitment of consequence.
People prefer to hide behind a superficial image of neu-
trality with regard to their own affairs.

But these very same people will manipulate and pull

strings, as long as they don't have to show themselves during the process of exposing others. The *modus operandi* is to bring the point across by thoroughly exploring the other point of view. Subsequently it will be discussed in ways that generate confusion and doubt. Such behavior is typical of people who suffer spiritual agony.

Genuine search for truth respects other points of view. This is how foundations for deeper understanding are built. But at the same time we must beware of presumptuous teaching and claims which lack reality and evidence. This warning also applies to religion, where issues must be examined in light of Scripture and reason. Therefore, let us discuss new concepts, like fundamentalism, and not fear proliferation or division in Christianity because of them.

God constantly reveals Himself through the activity of the Holy Spirit who, Christ says, "will glorify me, for he will take what is mine and declare it to you." (John 16:14) Thus, the truth about God is a daily revelation.

In this revelation of the truth about God, the Bible is a tool of the Holy Spirit. In its true spiritual sense, the Bible is a God-and-people book that relates the interaction of a righteous God and sinful people.

The truth of the Word of God is so important that its purpose is made known by the Holy Spirit for any specific need at hand. This precludes all human ambition to manipulate Biblical literature for speculative purposes. Nor should it become a mechanism to control faith in people.

Quite often, the sacred term "Word of God" is used interchangeably for Biblical literature. This substitution is wrong. The Word, or Logos, is the creative and sustaining Spirit of God as revealed in Jesus Christ (John 1). The Word of God is supreme. Within the doctrine of the Word, Biblical literature has a fourth-place position after the reality of God, Jesus Christ, and the revealed and spoken

Word. For example, the Word of God demands faithfulness
and obedience of people; Biblical literature tells about the
results and God's intent in future dealings because of humanity's disobedience.

Minor ecclesiastical problems—like fundamentalism—
only point to the much bigger problem that affects the
personal relationship between God and people. The overriding issue at hand is an identity crisis. This is a spiritual
problem.

We cannot hide from it by clouding the issue. Individuals, families, and even society as a whole have been reluctant or afraid for too long to find out the purpose of existence in light of whose we truly are.

As long as people choose to live in a state of aimless drift,
confusion will persist. This becomes further complicated
when groups within the Christian confession fail to stand
up and declare their faith in Christ or, worse yet, do not
live up to what they confess.

The relationship of God and people is not an issue of lofty
philosophical precepts, but is a way of life for all people, as
God has ordained it in creation and confirmed in redemption.

3

Life in the World Despite
the Other Person

God has created the human race as the means by which the Holy Spirit can work His will on earth. Therefore, as people of God, we are instruments—in a real physical sense—of divine power for implementing and bringing about God's purpose for creation.

Within this context, the most important issue concerning life and status in the world is remembering the fact that we are dependent creatures of God. We are mortal beings. We experience life as a gift. God, who created life in us with the holy breath of His Spirit, continues to sustain this life as a matter of grace. Creation and redemption are God's mark of ownership.

God cares for each person individually. There are no collective bargaining units in the Kingdom of God. Each soul must give its own account of stewardship in life.

The intimate relationship between God and people is a personal matter. Responsibility and accountability is strictly an affair between an individual and God. God's expectations of faithfulness and obedience rule out apologies for poor performance or lack of faith. We will not get away with excuses like overwhelming pressures, over-burdening circumstances, or pesty people to explain our ill behavior.

The record book of life on earth does not have margins

for qualifying our actions. We cannot explain away our responses, for life is a gift from God. We must use it! Lamenting about unfortunate circumstances that may have "forced" us to react in a certain way will not work.

At the Day of Judgment, Christ will review our life's journey in the world on the basis of our faith alone. When we receive the invitation to the eternal feast in heaven, only then will we know that our life of faithfulness and obedience has been blessed for the return to its rightful place among the heavenly host. The life we then will experience is restored fellowship with God.

In the moment of our salvation, God's claim on our life is permanently secured. We have not earned this privilege. It is ours because of God's righteousness. It will be bestowed because we have lived by grace in the steadfast promise that God through Christ will save us.

The fact of eternal peace in the presence of God rests on the promise by Christ that faithful believers already are united with Him. Our presence before Almighty God is secured, for that is where Christ dwells.

Our hope for eternal life, and the reality of a living relationship with God on earth, is anchored in the revealed truth of the Word of God that is made known to us in Cross and Gospel.

As Christians, we are God's instruments to witness to the world about what God has done. In this mission, we are "like light for the whole world," and are told to let this "light so shine before men, that they may see your good works and give glory to your Father who is in heaven." (Matthew 5:16)

There is nothing magical or mysterious about human life on earth. Nor need this life be confusing or darkened by fear or doubts. Spiritual needs and physical necessities are provided for by God. And the conditions for rewarding spiritual performance have been successfully demonstrated in the model of the godly life of Jesus Christ.

As additional guidance, we benefit from Christ's summary of God's expectations. The essence of the two Great Commandments imply the commitment of love, faithfulness, and obedience: "You shall love the Lord your God with all your heart, and with all your soul, and with all your strength, and with all your mind; and your neighbor as yourself." (Luke 10:27)

But the harsh reality of worldly existence proves life different from God's expectations. Unfortunately, only a few faithful and obedient believers remain for being chosen as instruments of the Holy Spirit. These will have to shoulder the load of giving continuous witness to the grace of God.

As dedicated Christians, we are spiritually set apart from the rest of the sinful world, although physically we are an active part in the world. But we are not alone. God is fully supportive by providing means and message through the Holy Spirit. Therefore, we can survive the hazardous environment of the world. Endurance is the key.

Christ forewarned the 70 disciples about hardships they would encounter in their witness on behalf of God's Kingdom: "I send you out as lambs in the midst of wolves." (Luke 10:3) This realistic assessment serves as a warning. It corrects any anticipation we may have about glorious self-satisfaction when we let the Holy Spirit work the will of God through us.

Living in the world today is not that much different from 2000 years ago when the Son of God walked the earth. The wickedness in the world continues despite the repeated lessons in history. Even though the world may violently reject our life of witness to the truth about God, we must remain steadfast and live in the fear of God and not be afraid of people.

Therefore, let us always remember that we exist in the world to bring glory to God. And we must do this despite the other person.

In our work of witness, we have only one obligation and that is to be completely faithful to the LORD. The rest of the unbelieving world is also God's creation, but as servants of God we have neither authority nor any need to speculate about God's purpose for other people around us. Preoccupation with personal views on life must not interfere with the work God wants to get done.

The evil in human nature always compels people to search for answers that are really none of their business; Christians are no exceptions. We also feel the urge to satisfy our curiosity by questioning God why "he makes his sun rise on the evil and on the good, and sends rain on the just and on the unjust." (Matthew 5:45)

Christ puts a stop to this by reminding us that a Christian's way of life deals with faithfulness and obedience to God. Toward this end Christ supports the believer with guidance: "You, therefore, must be perfect, as your heavenly Father is perfect." (Matthew 5:48)

But such straightforward spiritual truth may not always be satisfying to human beings. In an attempt to vent frustrating emotions, people will press on with unwarranted demands to have a more decisive voice in God's plan for the universe. Sin is more enticing than recognizing the purpose of our creation and yielding to God in faithfulness and obedience.

And this is precisely the dilemma of Christians, who are also emotionally charged human beings. Only when we as Christians realize that faithfulness and obedience to God implies that people have no choice in the matter of God's generosity and grace will personal frustrations and feelings of injustice vanish. Then within the fellowship of believers, we will have ample cause to rejoice that God has chosen to treat all people equally.

But our reluctance to witness to sinful people about the grace of God in Christ Jesus can complicate matters. The prophet Jeremiah bemoaned this particular problem: "Righteous art thou, O LORD, when I complain to thee; yet I would plead my case before thee. Why does the way of the wicked prosper? Why do all who are treacherous thrive?" (Jeremiah 12:1)

Christianity is not immune to attacks by ruthless people who work the rule of injustice, wickedness, and dishonesty. Therefore, as disciples of Christ we must speak out against these evils in the world. God demands our obedience by living the Gospel in a way that does not leave room for confusion but clarifies God's expectations in an affirmative way.

Failure to proclaim Cross and Gospel as an inseparable entity—the way God has intended it—only adds to the severity of today's identity crisis. The real working relationship with God is undermined whenever ecclesiastical theology chooses to emphasize primarily the Gospel portion of God's redeeming grace without pointing to the Cross, which made the glorious Easter message possible in the first place.

In Christ's call to follow him, the promise of new life depends on repentance, giving further proof of the Gospel's dependence on the Cross. Jesus Christ cried out: "The time is fulfilled, and the kingdom of God is at hand; repent, and believe in the gospel." (Mark 1:15) With the command to believe the Good News, we are specifically told to rid ourselves first from all sins so that we can become free in the Spirit, and then enjoy to our pure heart's delight the blessing of restored fellowship with God.

St. Paul addresses this specific issue of repentance and the subsequent commitment of faithfulness and obedience to God: "What shall we say then? Are we to continue in sin that grace may abound? By no means! How can we who died to sin still live in it? Do you not know that all of us who have been baptized into Christ Jesus were baptized into his death? We were buried therefore with him by baptism into death, so that as Christ was raised from the dead by the glory of the Father, we too might walk in newness of life . ... . So you also must consider yourselves dead to sin and alive to God in Christ Jesus. Let not sin therefore reign in your mortal bodies, to make you obey their passions." (Romans 6:1-4,11-12)

As we specifically look at the problem of the other person, we soon will learn that the "other person" really comprises all the forces of darkness. Rampant evil and raw sinfulness are only a few of the hindrances that Christians in the world must overcome in proving their steadfastness in the faith. Some of these barriers are prejudice and pride within ourselves, and we are confronted with the challenge to break them down.

Or, as with the prophet Jeremiah, we may be asked to witness to the grace of God to all people, despite injustice, wickedness, and dishonesty.

Christians have a duty to help correct these and other social ills. But we must also give support when integrity and dignity are attacked by ridicule, sarcasm, and scorn. And we are available to help ease the pain when relationships explode because of broken trust, rumors, or insinuations.

We can go on with an endless listing of general examples,

for evil does not recognize boundaries or limits. Some mental cruelty or physical abuse defies the vocabulary, as there are no words in existence to describe the evil that strains the human spirit to the breaking point.

In all situations of human stress, the only constructive recourse in dealing with "the other person" is to remember that as Christians we live in the world by the grace of God despite the other person. Elisha's prophetic declaration of confidence in God is appropriate in the face of doom: "Don't be afraid . . . we have more on our side than they have on theirs." (2 Kings 6:16)TEV

4

Surviving Trials and Temptations

There are no substitutes for faithfulness and obedience to God. Nevertheless, God has ordained universal salvation—the return to the proper place of eternal fellowship with God for all people—as a gift of grace. No one, therefore, will have valid reasons to try to outdo another person, deny equality to any people, or feel compelled to labor for salvation.

All Christians are children of God through union with Christ. Since the foundation of divine grace is the righteousness of God, Jesus Christ is like a cornerstone in the believer's heart. Christians now have the perfect opportunity to build their faith and grow in the hope of eternal life.

As part of potential and growth, we have the Holy Spirit of God living within believers. The divine Helper supports all efforts in faithfulness and obedience. Without the guidance from the Holy Spirit, faithfulness and obedience is more like a curse. It will enslave people in "good works."

So let us remember that life in the presence of God—through Christian discipleship—is a matter of faith and trust in God alone. As we practice our faith in God, faithfulness and obedience prove a blessing.

The Christian approach to life is faith and trust in God. We then follow up with good works, because we know to whom we truly belong.

But there are definite expectations that God has of Chris-

tians. Demands of faithfulness and obedience as contained
in the Law of Moses were not done away with. When
Christ confirmed their continuity in the Great Commandment, he elevated faithfulness and obedience to God to the
highest level in relationships: "You shall love the Lord your
God with all your heart, and with all your soul, and with all
your mind." (Matthew 22:37) Christians are charged to live
and work under the banner of love. Christ has given faithfulness and obedience a new meaning within the context of
God's message in the Gospel. Christ's teaching about the
Word of God now guides believers for attaining new
heights in our appreciation of God's work.

The meaning of truth within the Word of God is a matter
of constant revelation by the Holy Spirit. We will receive
guidance for specific needs as they arise—God has never
been limited by time or place.

Biblical literature provides continuity. It is the tool used
by the Holy Spirit to make known the truth about God.

But to share the Holy Spirit's revelation of divine truth
demands a firm commitment. We must acknowledge our
dependence on God the Spirit in order to overcome trials
and temptations.

Failure to recognize our spiritual oneness (John 14:20-26)
with God only proves that a faith relationship with God has
not been established. It shows that God is not acknowledged as the authority of all that exists.

This sad condition, so prevalent among many people in
the world today, relegates the subjects of faithfulness and
obedience as abstract ideas to different schools in philosophy. But abstract thought has neither place nor value in the
relationship with God.

Thus, faithfulness and obedience are rewarding and
meaningful only when confessing believers start and finish
daily activities in full realization of spiritual dependence on

God. Any "good works" will automatically take on substance because we strive to bring glory to God.

The meaning of faithfulness, obedience, trials, and temptations must therefore be viewed in light of God's message in the Gospel. Within this setting, we have a new "context story" about human behavior in spiritual encounters with the living God. New Testament writings in the Bible describe for Christians expectations and involvement.

The Bible details the dynamic relationship of a righteous God and sinful people. Christians live in obedience to the Holy Spirit, who alone can make known the truth of the Word of God for the specific need at hand.

Because the interaction with God is an individual matter, Christians need not feel obligated to supply proof of faith to other people. Nor is there a need for Christians to explain their spiritual dependence on God for life and support. It suffices to state that the spiritual reality between God and believer is demonstrated in prayer, where matters of importance are dealt with on the basis of personal faith and divine promise.

The makeup of the total person is the delicate combination of flesh and spirit. To understand ourselves more clearly, we must evaluate each other's contribution to overall well-being. When this is done in light of Christ's teaching, we will arrive at the conclusion that the spirit is in control despite selfish claims of human nature that only physical substance has meaning in the world.

As practicing Christians, let us not fall victim to false appetites of satisfying only physical existence. A strictly worldly outlook on life will make people selfish, greedy, proud, arrogant, conceited, and boastful.

Undoubtedly, there will always be huge audiences in the world to admire and applaud successful achievers—independent of the cost of success. But the Word of God is clear that success in the world is worthless, and people oriented only toward materialism are an eternal failure spiritually. This message is given in Jeremiah's prophecy against Moab: "We have heard of the pride of Moab—he is very proud—of his loftiness, his pride, and his arrogance, and the haughtiness of his heart. I know his insolence, says the LORD; his boasts are false, his deeds are false." (Jeremiah 48:29-30)

Because uncommitted people already swim in everlasting despair—though physically this horror is masked by worldly comforts and pleasures—they have no remorse. Since there is no conscience left, pain and agony about straining the spiritual relationship with God do not exist. A relationship had either never been formed in the first place, or was destroyed when pride and arrogance hardened the grooves of sin.

The temptation is there for our efforts to become diluted by arguments in logic or emotional issues. When this happens, our faith is on trial, and we must demonstrate what we believe. Friendships with humanistic-type people can be devastating to those who are weak in faith.

Humanism and materialism are not the only concerns. Because of the false assumption that all outward human expressions are an indication of inner beliefs and commitments, Christianity has suffered its share of wolves in sheep's clothing. Even seeing a person going to church each Sunday and performing great religious theatrics in speech and manner during the week does not necessarily set that person apart as a Christian saint. Hypocrites have always existed. They were scorned by John the Baptist in the call to repentance, and they were condemned by Christ.

Therefore, life in the real world is in constant danger. Foremost among them is lack of confidence. We are too polite in presenting those around us with God's truth in Cross and Gospel. And, of course, there are the hypocrites, who always manage to profess what they are not.

But all is not lost as long as we recognize ourselves as Christian saints because of God's righteousness and grace. Then, by the power of God, we will survive all onslaught of evil in the world. As we additionally realize that we are real people in the world and not perfect saints, our humility as struggling sinners will help prepare the way for God's forgiveness and love.

As long as there is a world, the people living in it will always be the explosive combination of saint and sinner.

History has already proven this as a fact of life. Any realistic view of life, therefore, requires that we accept what we are, yet always remembering that we owe it to ourselves to strive for the better way of life ordained by God.

Because the makeup of human beings, good and bad alike, is all part of God's creation, people will be able to achieve a spiritually satisfying life in the presence of God despite the sinfulness of human nature. God made this possible through a life in union with Christ.

But this newness of life that God has based totally on divine righteousness and provided as a matter of grace nonetheless demands our response and a firm commitment.

Thus, whenever we find ourselves at the crossroads of life, we must resolve the personal challenge of declaring our allegiance, similar to the call for allegiance that God had demanded through Moses of the Israelites in their journey to the promised land: "I call heaven and earth to witness against you this day, that I have set before you life and death, blessing and curse; therefore choose life, that you and your descendants may live, loving the LORD your

God, obeying his voice, and cleaving to him; for that means life to you . . . ." (Deuteronomy 30:19-20)

But once the commitment to God is made, then trials and temptations will also start to set in. Satan, as a foe of God and the accuser of mankind, is determined to break the bond of restored fellowship with God, and prove to God, once again, that the sinfulness of mankind is not any different from the spiritual sinfulness of the first man Adam.

There is no worldly comparison for a person's spiritual anguish of trials and temptations. For example, we may hear other people talk about being tempted to go to the races or finding themselves on trial because they have overspent their budget. All such concerns deal with temporal life. As Christians, however, we know that we exist beyond the immediate and don't belong to ourselves. When we leave this world, we live on because we are God's children. Trials and temptations involve us as a matter of doing what God wants.

The makeup of the present day saint-sinner is similar to that of ancient mankind. But our spiritual opportunities are different, because of what God through Christ did 2000 years ago.

For example, we see in Genesis that Abraham was an ordinary man. He put to use his multiple talents in the handling of many conflicts. But the truly outstanding feature in the life of Abraham was a wholehearted commitment to God.

This gave him strength to cope when deciding many choices. It guided him in handling the boundary dispute with his nephew Lot (Genesis 13:8-9); it gave him courage to rescue Lot and his family from a raiding party (Genesis 14:1-16); it proved him compassionate as he bargained with God to spare the people of Sodom (Genesis 18:16-33); it gave him vision to see God in the visitation of three angels (Genesis 18:1-5).

But Abraham also was a man of the world. He tried to save his own skin when he passed off Sarah as his sister and let her be picked by the Egyptian Pharaoh for his harem (Genesis 12:10-20). God's intervention saved an unscrupulous liar. Abraham had great spiritual depth, but he also was a person with common weaknesses and needs.

The highlighted events in Abraham's life resemble the general nature of the conflicts which all generations commonly experience. We also have the best of intentions in overcoming evil and hardship, but we are not always successful in achieving this goal. And many times we must struggle to keep our priorities straight; undoubtedly, Abraham must have felt similar frustrations.

Yet, as Christ's followers, we live in the hope of eternal life, as God is presiding over the miracle that alone is capable of redeeming the worst of sinners.

Therefore, let us thoroughly understand the nature of our being within the environment that God has placed us in, and examine our existence in terms of Cross and Gospel. Doing so will help us to better cope with the stress that any proof of our faith may force upon us.

A thorough review will soon reveal that any direct involvement in trials and temptations is not necessarily a sign of weakness in faith or character of the person exposed to trial's anguish and pain. Like Job in his trial, Christians may also find themselves just like an article of trade in the enmity between God and Satan.

We must remain steadfast in our faith despite the cosmic conflict around us in which the forces of light and darkness battle for the souls of people. We will fail in our commitment whenever we decide to rely on our own strength to win the victory over trials and temptations.

Thus, we must constantly keep before us the blessing of God's grace. Boastful self-reliance only proves our foolishness and will make us unfaithful and disobedient toward God. We will receive strength to survive trials and temptations by seeking God's help under the guidance of the Holy Spirit.

Because temptations to make people sin will not lessen, as Christians we must practice constant alert. In his objective to destroy the life-sustaining relationship with God, Satan very proficiently will gnaw at physical well-being with the tools of sickness, disease, and even death, to raise doubts in the minds of believers for a change of heart in the matter of allegiance to God. Less dramatic attacks by Satan are character assassinations through lies. It is a common occurrence that the faithful must defend character and integrity against rumors and gossip.

Yet, as people of God we live in the world to bring glory to God's Kingdom, despite adverse conditions, frightening circumstances, and pesty people. We have neither power nor authority to deal with Satan's legions in the world, but neither do we have any right to hide like an ostrich from trials and temptations. We must face up to the baited traps of Satan, but not with our own strength and the wits of the human mind. Even to consider that we have the ability to do so may be fatal to us.

Only by the power of the Word of God can we survive trials and overcome temptations. Help from God is readily available, as Christ specifically has taught us in the petition of the Lord's Prayer, "lead us not into temptation, but deliver us from evil." (Matthew 6:13)

As we realize whose we are, we will then also find reason to boast about God's redeeming grace. The fact is that we are redeemed and "justified by faith, we have peace with God through our Lord Jesus Christ. Through him we have obtained access to this grace in which we stand, and we rejoice in our hope of sharing the glory of God." (Romans 5:1-2)

As a true servant of God, Christ was faithful and obedient. He did not react with emotional outbursts or arrogant displays of knowledge, but was specific in quoting the authority of the Word of God.

Inasmuch as Christ relied totally on God's power and accepted the authority of the Father, so we as Christians likewise must yield to the authority of God. To do otherwise will place us in opposition to God and make believers ready prey for Satan.

The petition, "lead us not into temptation, but deliver us from evil" (Matthew 6:13), is truly heard and answered by God when a Christian's witness echoes the inspiration authored by the Holy Spirit living in us: "I am a Christian—through Christ I belong to God!"

5

Knowledge, Truth, Theories, and Opinions

No models exist in the world to demonstrate inspiration. Even Christ's parables give only glimpses as to what heaven is like. Through them Christ just barely touches eternal truth to make things understandable. Whereas other people must speculate about what is important in life, in spiritual vision God invites believers to share divine inspirations.

Spiritual matters cannot be comprehended in terms of conventional knowledge. Only the Holy Spirit of God can guide believers properly through moments of visionary truth whenever God's creation waits prepared to unfold its panoramic splendor.

When Christ told the disciples, "I have yet many things to say to you, but you cannot bear them now" (John 16:12), he was telling those who believe that there is no way for them to grasp and retain all at once what there is to know about the truth of the Word of God, but that the truth about God is given through continuous revelation by the Holy Spirit.

We must recall that as instruments of the Holy Spirit, we are the means of God's grace to fill specific needs. Thus, we must be faithful and obedient in our service of making known the living God to all people in the world.

God has not created humans to be intellectual geniuses

33

or speculative philosophers. The mission of Christian discipleship is defined as faithful and obedient service. Believers are like light for the world and bring glory to God.

But the curiosity in human nature always wants to venture out in search of answers. We are quickly intrigued by
far-out subjects. There is no limit to fantasy.

Despite a genuine desire to gain knowledge, we have
less interest in a deeper appreciation of God's obligation for
mankind. Faithfulness and obedience to God, therefore,
are looked at from a distance.

There is a general problem with organized religion.
Throughout history, doctrines and dogmas were used as
tools to force the membership to conform to church policy.
And ecclesiastical theology has intimidated many gifted
minds in the search for truth.

It was quite common in history for the church to dictate
truth. Sometimes those in control even compromised their
spiritual dependence on God for the sake of satisfying
personal ambition.

History reveals the repudiation by the church of Copernicus' heliocentric theory. The events of that time specifically highlight the agony felt by gifted people, like
Copernicus (1473-1543), who in addition to being an as-
tronomer and mathematician also was a devout churchman.

About a century later, Copernicus' propositions precipitated the clash between science and the church. Religious
groups extracted Biblical "evidence" to back their claims
that God had worked the creation of the universe according
to a geocentric blueprint. The Roman Catholic Church
rejected Copernicus' proposals. His writing "Revolutions"
was declared as "false and altogether opposed to Holy
Scriptures" and it was blacklisted in the church's "Index
Librorum Prohibitorum."

Copernicus' courage opened the way for in-depth study of truth which has carried over to this day as evidenced by scholarship in academia and objectivity in our dealings with everyday issues. But as with all acts of greatness, the fight against ignorance is also costly. Copernicus and workers after him had to risk life, fortune, and exposure to ridicule.

Such impact was felt by Galileo (1564-1642) who suffered the brunt of the church's wrath when he dared to stand up for truth. This practical man and a genius of mechanics was the perfect complement to the theoretical Johann Kepler (1571-1630) who, among other laws, also had formulated the harmonic law of planetary motion. Galileo's precision in experiment and observation confirmed him a champion of truth. But this dedication cost him dearly. In a statement prepared for him, he was forced to denounce his accomplishments before a tribunal of the Inquisition.

These events in the development of planetary theories deserve our attention today because they exemplify the need for perseverance in the search and defense of truth. This is how freedom through knowledge is gained.

Whenever the combination of knowledge and truth is manipulated, there is a tight control over the lives of people. Suffering and death because of poverty and starvation is the fruit of ignorance that is caused by ruthless individuals in control of so-called truth and right opinions. Economic pressure is used as a common tool to enforce conformity.

But this is not the only problem in the world. Another form of chaos is generated by some people who are best described as preoccupied "scholars." These thinkers will influence social behavior with new speculations about the purpose and meaning of human life.

Yet the life-long obsession of freethinkers has seldom

produced a lasting contribution to society. If anything, their substitute for God's demand for faithfulness and obedience has impeded harmony among people.

The freethinker is a modern product of sophistication and false teaching. Whenever human imagination stresses the truth about God, and subsequently insists on these ideas as doctrine, people will respond as skeptics, agnostics, and nonbelievers to question that particular ideology.

Freethinkers live as if God did not exist—sometimes this also is true of people who claim to be Christians. Therefore, in terms of social behavior, the dividing line is not clear. Some freethinkers will consent to the existence of an "ultimate power" and unwittingly work the Golden Rule (Matthew 7:12) with greater ambition than the lipservice of some "Christians." But the fact is that freethinkers live only for the satisfaction of earthly goals and then die.

When those around us fail to see God in Christ, this is an indictment of Christian witness. Truth is further clouded by some "Christians"—mostly sectarian in character—who insist that their teaching is the only correct way of believing. Even the assertion about the infallibility of the papacy and worldly religious councils is diluting truth. As a modern concept, therefore, atheism will exist as long as there is an audience (2 Timothy 4:3)—and idolatrous Christianity keeps building the stage by neglecting sound doctrine (Titus 2:1-3:7).

The Psalmist writes, "The fool says in his heart, 'There is no God'" (Psalms 14:1), thereby pointing to the rejection of God as the highest folly. We must help people overcome this foolishness, for God is always near to take sinners back. Fear commonly prompts moments of truth. Soldiers tell us in stories about battlefield conditions that there is never an atheist in a foxhole.

The failure of human ideas as a substitute for belief and

trust in God is exposed in Marxist theories and their brand of socialism: Totalitarian governments must use force to subdue people in order to make communism work.

Each generation has its share of imaginative people. There is never a shortage of dreams. But when unproven methods start to influence people, confusion is further compounded.

We are reluctant to really seek the truth about God. We are too slow to increase in spiritual stature.

Christ has clearly stated: "If you continue in my word, you are truly my disciples, and you will know the truth, and the truth will make you free." (John 8:31-32) But somehow it appears that the laws governing the ecclesiastical affairs of a Christian church have more power over people than the truth about God.

As Christians we already know whose we are and what we once were. It behooves us, nevertheless, to refresh our memories concerning the truth of the Word of God. The writer of Proverbs offered advice to young men that is appropriate for all children of God: "The fear of the LORD is the beginning of knowledge; fools despise wisdom and instruction." (Proverbs 1:7)

He then continues to make truth applicable to real-life situations: "Trust in the LORD with all your heart, and do not rely on your own insight. In all your ways acknowledge him, and he will make straight your paths." (Proverbs 3:5-6)

As we experience the love of God that is grace, the wisdom literature from Proverbs projects eternal truth as the reality of life: "My son, do not despise the LORD's discipline or be weary of his reproof, for the LORD reproves him whom he loves, as a father the son in whom he delights." (Proverbs 3:11-12)

But such simple truth is not always satisfying to people.

Human nature is more intrigued about the complex. Whatever sounds more complicated is more appealing. Far-out concepts invite speculations.

Therefore, people will readily venture into classical philosophy in search of answers for their lives. This is done despite the fact that classical philosophy must be viewed within the framework of its ancient culture. But this is not at all upsetting to those who feel satisfied to borrow tidbits of information here and there and make certain catchwords their new theme.

Against all these spiritual alternatives stands the Word of God. Its only demand is that we lose ourselves in Christ if we want to avoid an identity crisis in our lives.

There is constant danger that we all may become exposed to spiritual degeneration at some point in our lives. Therefore, we must train ourselves to recognize pitfalls that could make us sin. The fact is that sin—missing the mark in our relationship with God—destroys spiritual discernment in the lives of people.

Sin brought about the downfall of the kingdoms of Israel and Judah. Sinful behavior also permeated the apostolic church. This happened despite the fact that the charge was clearly defined: "Let all the house of Israel therefore know assuredly that God has made him both Lord and Christ, this Jesus whom you crucified . . . And there is salvation in no one else, for there is no other name under heaven given among men by which we must be saved." (Acts 2:36, 4:12)

Christianity, therefore, is not immune to attacks, even though Christianity is a covenant relationship with the living God. This new covenant was consummated by God at Golgatha and its essence is preserved for all posterity in Cross and Gospel.

As Christians, we are individually responsible to carry on Christ's witness to make known the living God to all people in the world. In evidence of commitment and dedication to God, we must live a life of truth. Failure to do so carries dire consequences.

Even though we recognize the essence of Christianity as the one eternal truth and the one universal salvation, ecclesiastical religion, partly due to factionalism, has many times failed to live up to God's expectations. This is visible in the world wherever Cross and Gospel are separated in witnessing and teaching.

In God's plan for human salvation, the Cross of Christ is the redeeming element of grace. Its reality is also the means by which God reminds believers that the curse of the law (Deuteronomy 21:23) is transformed into a blessing of faith. To this truth St. Paul gives testimony: "Christ redeemed us from the curse of the law, having become a curse for us—for it is written, 'Cursed be every one who hangs on a tree'—that in Christ Jesus the blessing of Abraham might come upon the Gentiles, that we might receive the promise of the Spirit through faith." (Galatians 3:13-14)

The Gospel is the vehicle for proclaiming this truth and extends an invitation to all people to assemble beneath the Cross so that believers may by its light and shadow give proper witness in service to God and people. St. Paul speaks of the power of the Cross: "Christ did not send me to baptize but to preach the gospel, and not with eloquent wisdom, lest the cross of Christ be emptied of its power. For the word of the cross is folly to those who are perishing, but to us who are being saved it is the power of God." (1 Corinthians 1:17-18)

Christ suffered and died for the forgiveness of sins. And Christ died for the sins of people once and for all. This is the truth of the Cross. And the truth of the Gospel is the glorious Easter message in which God has declared that all who believe in Christ share through his death on the Cross his resurrection in the hope of eternal life.

Any confusion created by overzealous ecclesiastical religion is due to the emphasis placed primarily on the Gospel. Apparently that is the easier sales pitch. People want everything that has to do with their well-being, without having to be reminded that the Cross made the Gospel possible in the first place.

In other words, idolatrous Christianity wants to bask in the Gospel on Sunday without having to carry the Cross from Monday through Saturday.

Under this set of circumstances, Christianity is courting idol worship. Christianity is drawn into this problem because of people who say they are Christians since they happen to go to church each Sunday. Yet during weekdays these people serve themselves instead of glorifying God in Christ.

Christian conduct means that we are prepared to help people in need. If this is not so, we expose Christ to ridicule and scorn. Sometimes this is the case especially in the competitive atmosphere of the workplace. The sheep of Sundays are raving wolves on weekdays. In every instance where faith is not practiced, Christianity is victimized by hypocrites. As human needs are then satisfied by nonbelievers, worldly humanism gains and the Kingdom of God loses. Therefore, let all confessing Christians beware! Christ projects condemnation for our failure to take care of needy people (Matthew 25:31-46).

This problem has existed throughout the ages. And it will not easily go away, however hard Christians may try in witnessing to the truth of the Word of God.

God's charge to the prophet Ezekiel firms up the charge regarding our involvement in witnessing: "If I say to the wicked, 'You shall surely die,' and you give him no warning, nor speak to warn the wicked from his wicked way, in order to save his life, that wicked man shall die in his iniquity; but his blood I will require at your hand. But if you warn the wicked, and he does not turn from his wickedness, or from his wicked way, he shall die in his iniquity; but you will have saved your life. Again, if a righteous man turns from his righteousness and commits iniquity, and I lay a stumbling block before him, he shall die; because you have not warned him, he shall die for his sin, and his righteous deeds which he has done shall not be remembered; but his blood I will require at your hand. Nevertheless if you warn the righteous man not to sin, and he does not sin, he shall surely live, because he took warning; and you will have saved your life." (Ezekiel 3:18-21)

Thus, Christians are individually responsible for the truth in witnessing and teaching. Christ said: "but whoever causes one of these little ones who believe in me to sin, it would be better for him to have a great millstone fastened around his neck and to be drowned in the depth of the sea. Woe to the world for temptations to sin! For it is necessary that temptations come, but woe to the man by whom the temptation comes!" (Matthew 18:6-7)

Whenever the truth of Cross and Gospel is split and our witnessing only emphasizes the truth of the Gospel, then the power of the Word of God is reduced to a weak appeal. An indecisive witness to the grace of God in salvation will mislead people by giving them the false impression that once the Gospel is received, people now have a license to do what they want because they believe that the grace of God is working for them. Nothing is further from the truth!

To be sure, salvation is by grace through faith alone "and there is salvation in no one else, for there is no other name under heaven given among men by which we must be saved." (Acts 4:12) But we must understand that this truth of the Gospel is dependent on the Cross. We find the combined truth of Cross and Gospel summarized in the prophecy of Ezekiel to the Israelites: "Therefore I will judge you, O house of Israel, every one according to his ways, says the LORD GOD. Repent and turn from all your transgressions, lest iniquity be your ruin. Cast away from you all the transgressions which you have committed against me, and get yourselves a new heart and a new spirit! Why will you die, O house of Israel? For I have no pleasure in the death of any one, says the LORD GOD; so turn, and live." (Ezekiel 18:30-32)

And Jesus Christ confirmed the call of repentance by John the Baptist, saying: "The time is fulfilled, and the kingdom of God is at hand; repent, and believe in the gospel." (Mark 1:15) And Christ, indeed, has come to fulfill both Law and Prophets.

Now we need not speculate further and follow ancient ways of thinking as passed down by classical philosophy, for the Holy Spirit of God is living among us to reveal the truth about God. Nor do we need a philosophy of human conduct—including the much-honored precepts of classical ethics—for the personal relationship of the redeemed with the living God has the Law of God imprinted on the believer's hearts in the form of the Cross.

Therefore, with regard to human knowledge, let us use the mind to further the glory of God and be "like light for the whole world." We have the God-given obligation to be ambitious in the full development and utilization of God's power in creation through all the channels of science—physics, chemistry, biology, mathematics, etc.—or industry in farming and manufacturing or life-supporting endeavors like medicine.

Yet, in all these efforts, we must remember that the

spirit has superiority over the flesh, for "God is spirit, and those who worship him must worship in spirit and truth." (John 4:24)

Thus we remember that our spiritual being started with Adam and was confirmed in Abraham. The Father of Many Nations, Abraham was the first to receive what God has promised, and he indeed is the father of faith for the three great monotheistic religions: Judaism, Christianity, and Islam. "And he believed the LORD; and he reckoned it to him as righteousness." (Genesis 15:6)

But the evil in human nature is prominent whenever the truth about God is manipulated by worldly intelligence. These unfortunate happenings are truly trying moments for those dedicated to God as indidividuals or the church as the fellowship of believers.

6

A Matter of Economics

The human race, as the choice of God's creation, has been blessed to share spiritual oneness with God. Restored fellowship with God was made possible through a life of union with Christ.

Yet despite God's offer of grace in universal salvation, people continue to undermine this opportunity through selfishness, pride, and greed. They carry on as Adam did when he denied and rejected God's generosity.

And failure to recognize the presence of God in daily life continues even today to lead many people astray. In the resultant state of confusion, all uncommitted people, like Cain, are ideal candidates for God's concern.

Hence Biblical literature has preserved divine truth to act as guidance and direction for life: "The LORD said to Cain, 'Why are you angry, and why has your countenance fallen? If you do well, will you not be accepted? And if you do not do well, sin is couching at the door; its desire is for you, but you must master it.' " (Genesis 4:6-7)

Despite God's assessment of the evil in envy and greed, there still are many people in the world today who scorn knowledge and enlightenment through the truth of Christ's teaching. They continue a way of life similar to Cain's. He had great ambition to prove his humanity, but it condemned him to commit murder. Greed and envy over-

powered his senses. Cain had chosen a life in total ignorance of his spiritual identity.

Cain's calculating view of his relationship with the living
God had become formalized into a simple matter of economics. Whereas Abel dedicated himself to God when he
brought the first lamb born to one of his sheep, killed it,
and gave the best parts of it as an offering, Cain considered
some of his fruit harvest just fine for meeting the minimum
requirement for assurance of God's blessing and favor.

But God found only Abel's offering acceptable. Abel had
truly presented himself and committed his entire future
into God's hands.

This evidence shows that Abel knew God as a matter of
trust and that Abel relied on God to provide for all future
needs. But we also learn from the demise of Abel that
faithful and obedient people face danger whenever they
make known their commitment. History has proven over
and over again that the world has never suffered from a
shortage of Cains.

Greedy and envious people are in the world wherever
we go. They are part of a Christian's challenge to make
known the living God to all people in the world. This also
includes bringing the witness of divine grace in equal measure even to the Cains of this world.

Thus, Christ is telling all followers to carry their own
crosses when doing God's will in service to God and
people. The instructions are clear: "Let your light so shine
before men, that they may see your good works and give
glory to your Father who is in heaven." (Matthew 5:16)

Yet despite knowledge of Christ's commands to repent
and believe in the Gospel people continue to choose living
in the curse of Cain. Selfishness is driving these possessed
souls to the idol worship of accumulated wealth. And they
actually work themselves to death doing it.

As a result of this obsession, their greed has made them useless in doing the work of God, for there is not to be found among them even the slightest concern with the Kingdom of God and with what he requires. In its stead we see ruthless wielding of power whose foundation is not God but accumulated wealth.

We find these modern Cains exploiting other people by working the rule of getting the most for the least. They will remind those associated with them that it is a privilege to be working together. They are generous with sweet-talk. It does not cost them anything. Some even do it in full knowledge of any oppressive burdens they themselves have placed on others.

The poor and the destitute are relegated to subhuman levels of existence. There is little or no hope for the better way of life simply because all opportunities for advancement are viciously guarded, even the ones that people of influence and power administer as a matter of public trust.

Yet, like Cain, these arrogant "benefactors" of society scowl whenever they see the grace of God uplifting downtrodden spirits. They are jealous of happiness in others whenever the power of God's love is seen active and real. The glow of genuine brotherhood among poor but inspired people is seen in their sharing and caring for each other.

As the love of God is real among the faithful and the obedient, so is the anger of arrogant people, as they sense that their phony piety does not measure up to God's expectation that demands true love in return for grace.

Christ's teaching is clear that only those who live in a true state of sincere humility of the spirit will be able to share the Kingdom of heaven as rightful heirs together with Christ.

This promise of true happiness is witnessed to by Christ

in the Sermon on the Mount. Christ's promise is universal truth. It requires that we fully know our identity. We must recognize that the status of restored fellowship with God is based on the righteousness of God alone and handed to believers in Christ as a gift of grace. This eternal truth must be clearly established in our mind even before we attempt to refresh our memories about whose we truly are.

Only when Christians see each other as children of the true and living God can Christianity be acclaimed as containing the principles of the one eternal truth and the one universal salvation. Its members are "like light for the whole world."

Consequently, the Holy Spirit will use the dedicated hearts and willing minds of believers to work the power of God through them and make Christ's light shine so that other people "may see your good works and give glory to your Father who is in heaven." (Matthew 5:16)

Many people have not committed themselves to help the Kingdom of God on earth, for God does not force his will and expectation on anyone. Human beings have freedom of choice. A Christian's responsibility is clearly defined, but is a matter of personal commitment. We must learn all about God's expectation so that we can serve him more faithfully.

We must understand that as human beings in the world we live in constant conflict. We are torn between two diametrically opposed realities.

Yet we must remember that the spirit has superiority over the flesh, even though this may seem contrary to our physical nature. Thus, a spiritual treatment of life is indeed appropriate. Only the sinful human nature will want to see it otherwise and pretend to be in charge.

People who live according to worldly standards will want to push spiritual involvement aside. So we hear the scornful, though seemingly logical question: "What does the spirit have to do with the price of bananas?"

But as quickly as green bananas ripen and spoil, so will the short human pilgrimage on earth come to a sudden end.

This sad result will come about because people have failed to realize their spiritual identity. They have failed to recognize God's purpose for their lives.

Because human despair is an ultimate consequence of faithlessness, all hope for a better future has vanished. In their hopelessness people will see eternity fleeting right before their eyes.

There is no such thing as a second chance for recapturing time. Nor can the entries in the Book of Life be rewritten or amended by human effort.

Past experiences—good or bad alike—are history. Time is God's way of giving people a fresh beginning in preparation for meeting Christ on the Day of Judgment. Christians are told to let bygones be bygones: "No one who puts his hand to the plow and looks back is fit for the kingdom of God." (Luke 9:62)

Some people are more interested in raising their self-esteem within the realm of worldly affairs than being concerned above everything else with the Kingdom of God and with what he requires. They will protest that words with spiritual connotations are meaningless to them.

People whose only intentions for life are worldly considerations and involvement want to see the power of the Word of God reduced to the level where it will serve them. This reasoning is the biggest excuse for not wanting to make a commitment of dedication to God through Christ.

Like all other self-serving approaches to life, so is this unwarranted demand to make religion understandable nothing more than a trick. It has been in existence ever since the Church of the Pentecost celebration was formed; it wants to cheapen the grace of God by making religion more worldly. Yet there is no justification for lowering

God's expectations of faithful witness to Cross and Gospel. We must recognize that the Kingdom of God and the world are not meant to be reconciled, and that the Spirit has authority and power over the physical and emotional being of man.

The problem making it hard for people to maintain a decent standard of living is not always the "have" versus the "have not." Economic security is found in the ability of all people, rich and poor alike, to accept their status as children of God and labor in faith. We all share in the promise that God will provide.

To realize God's blessing, we must humble ourselves, and in the humility of our spirit sincerely desire to put our life in harmony with the will and purpose of God.

In the parable of the rich fool, Jesus warns all people that accumulated wealth cannot be transferred to heaven (Luke 12:16-20). True wealth is the hope of eternal life. We then rest our case in the knowledge that all faithful and obedient people will share with Christ in the glory of God. This is reserved for us at the end of our labors, for we, indeed, were concerned above everything else with the Kingdom of God and with what it requires (Matthew 6:33).

Therefore, whenever people feel overburdened by worldly difficulties, obvious issues on the surface are not always the root cause of the problems. It may appear that these alone strain human life to the breaking point and bring disaster on societies. We must search deeper and realize that the foundation of all life is spiritual.

Lack of faith in Christ is the root of all our problems. And by emphasizing only the worldly view of life, people contribute toward their own ignorance.

This fact is evident when people rely entirely on the expertise of the world, whose convincing arguments declare theories as fact. But theories seldom or never give any relief from oppression.

Yet people perpetuate this falsehood with their gullible attitudes. They clamor to hear what the world spoon-feeds. Instead we should search to know the truth about God. We must submit ourselves to the control of the Holy Spirit, who, Jesus said, "will guide you into all the truth." (John 16:13)

Truth is the solution to all tensions. It leads us to God so that divine power can work through us. Yet, we cannot expect a panacea. We must remember that we have submitted ourselves to God's care under God's condition.

Ignorance is a tool of Satan whereby he makes the rich poor and drives the poor to despair. Ignorance is best at covering its own ground. Its true identity will always be insidious and hidden. Hence confusion in the world will continue because priorities are scrambled.

Stressful situations bring out the animal instinct in people. People must struggle to survive. Any resultant psychological strain overloads emotional capacity to the breaking point, because people are suddenly forced to realize that their superficial faith is nothing more than wishful thinking.

Christianity is challenged to stand up, be counted, and lead people toward God. But Christians must also be concerned to right the wrong done to innocent victims, though they themselves may not feel the pain. Any silence only serves to approve the suffering of others.

If as Christians we fail to speak up and defend what is right, we are guilty of contributing to the tensions of others. For instance, this is the case when economic hardship is caused by deficit spending. We are involved and responsible when we approve the action of government to pay for any programs that may benefit us now, but whose debentures have dire consequences on the livelihood of future generations.

We rob our children of their potential in the future by

tapping this potential to pay our commitments. We are guilty of dragging future generations, not at all connected with our difficulties, into our specific predicaments.

We must remember that we alone are responsible, as well as accountable, for all our actions. Any relaxed attitudes toward deficit spending casts a shadow on the quality of our spiritual life.

Proponents of deficit spending may argue that at the time of a debt issue people will gain satisfaction from holding a bond instead of a tax receipt. This reasoning does not touch base with the harsh reality of life that only those people who can afford to buy government securities will gain the satisfaction of holding a money receipt instead of a paid tax bill.

The truth of the matter is that government borrowing transfers purchasing power to higher income groups. And those who cannot afford to buy bonds will suffer a far greater effect of higher prices—and higher interest rates— that the debt issue may have precipitated than the well-to-do. Already struggling families will experience little satisfaction from the privilege of retiring any debt issue by paying higher taxes.

The effect of inflation is felt by everyone—people and institutions alike. From 1953 to the 1970s people in the United States have seen the biggest inflation in history. During this period creeping inflation of 1-6% per year— some years even higher—has raised havoc with the best of intentions in budgeting and planning. Families are hurting to keep up with the cost of living.

How does the high cost of living create family problems? The issue goes beyond basic survival. We must look at the well-being of children in households where both parents are forced to work in order to cover expenses. The immediate effect is a generation of youth that has to raise itself. Is it then any wonder that such children are full of frustration, because there is no family outlet for their adventures in life?

Even if children manage to keep their stories bottled up till evening, they seldom will be heard as exhausted parents return from a hard day's work and don't want to be bothered with matters so seemingly insignificant as a child's greatest discovery in life.

And there are those who are left by the wayside. We see the retired, whose savings have evaporated as inflation has reduced the value of money. We find homes being confiscated for taxes. People cannot afford to live anymore in the residences they have legally paid for.

One of the greatest injustices occurs in industrialized society. It is not right to force a dedicated breadwinner in the prime of life into unemployment because a convenient reorganization has eliminated senior positions.

These tensions are real. Economic responsibility is so overwhelmingly misused that we do not have either power or authority to overcome it. But God does!

Excess wealth is not the only issue facing people. Responsible management of God's resources proves faithful stewardship. Our mission in life is to bring glory to God. But this cannot come about when we create tensions in others, or if we fail to condemn such practices by others.

7

The Bible

The Bible details the pilgrimage of mankind as a life of choice between two opposing realities. As such, it demonstrates the ongoing conflict between the cosmic power of light and darkness.

As people of God living in the world, Christians are part of the continuous battles between good and evil. We are exposed to suffering and pain as we struggle to overcome the conflict within our lives.

Accordingly, Biblical literature serves to remind people that life in all its relationships—with God and with other people—is precious to God. Our behavior is important to spiritual survival.

The control of emotions and physical aggressiveness is so crucial to personal well-being that God is specifically reminding people through Biblical literature about imminent judgment. Individuals will be held accountable for all actions on earth. Our failure to honor the sanctity of human life will influence the outcome of Christ's judgment and determine spiritual destiny. Life in all its relationships is sacred to God.

Jesus Christ has demonstrated the model of the godly life for us. Believers will become disciples when they follow Christ's example of faithfulness and obedience to God the Father.

What will often appear like a seemingly confusing future

of chaos and despair are nothing more than misleading impressions to discourage the uncommitted. Satan works to destroy the hope of those with little faith by keeping from them the penetrating rays of God's glory at the end of the tunnel of darkness. Discouragements are very effective tools of evil.

God has distinctly provided direction by means of the Bible's inspirational message. Its timeless truth is a matter of revelation through the Holy Spirit. But to make use of comfort and help from God requires that we accept God's offer of guidance. We must keep our lives in harmony with God's objectives.

Under the guiding support of God's Holy Spirit, faithful believers may draw on God's never-ending power for finishing Christ's work in the world. This life-sustaining blessing is recorded in the Bible as Christ's promise.

The Bible shows that the will of God on earth is accomplished through people. Thus, the relationship between God and people demands that believers become fruitful in their work on behalf of God's Kingdom, for the mission of human life on earth is to bring glory to God.

Christ's prophetic declaration identifies Christians as the visible means of God's glory—we are "like light for the whole world."

Hence restored fellowship with God is a divine gift that is unique to Christianity. Through it Christians contribute to the Kingdom of God on earth. We are taught that restored fellowship is established for the purpose of sustaining a faithful witness. God's saving presence strengthens believers so that the will and purpose of God in creation can be properly fulfilled.

The Bible tells about relationships. It talks about rebellion, rejection, greed, anger, and hate. But the Bible also tells us about love, precisely the love of God for sinful people: "For a brief moment I forsook you, but with great compassion I will gather you. In overflowing wrath for a moment I hid my face from you, but with everlasting love I will have compassion on you, says the LORD, your Redeemer." (Isaiah 54:7-8) The Bible makes the hope which grows out of repentance meaningful and real.

Repentant sinners can count on this assurance, because God's grace is based on divine righteousness alone and made available as a gift in fulfillment of God's promise: "For the mountains may depart and the hills be removed, but my steadfast love shall not depart from you, and my covenant of peace shall not be removed, says the LORD, who has compassion on you." (Isaiah 54:10)

God has reached out to sinful people solely on the basis of grace. But this divine offer for salvation requires that believers have faith in Christ as God's anointed Savior. This faith in Christ is made real and visible when contrite hearts urgently want to learn the will of God and then follow up all good intentions with commitment and dedication.

Biblical literature shows that the love of God has constantly reached out to people, independent of the many shortcomings of human nature. Repentant sinners can now share salvation through God's promise in Cross and Gospel—God's promise takes care of even the worst of sinners.

Consequently, the writer of the Gospel according to St. John describes the love of God as the force that alone can propel the human spirit into eternity: "For God so loved the world that he gave his only Son, that whoever believes in him should not perish but have eternal life." (John 3:16)

And Christianity, as the one form of universal salvation, teaches that eternal life is ordained by God as spiritual union with Christ and communion with God through Christ. For in God's Kingdom, Christ commands the rightful place as the authority of beginning and end: " 'I am the Alpha and the Omega,' says the Lord God, who is and who was and who is to come, the Almighty." (Revelation 1:8)

Contrary to popular notions, the Bible is not a book of magic for making people religious. Nor is the Bible a weapon of doctrine or traditions for controlling human behavior to make people conform to ecclesiastical policy.

If anything, the revealed message of Christ's teaching declares war, figuratively and in reality, on legions of people who are complacent with sinful traditions. Christ's prelude to the Gospel is a call for repentance: "The time is fulfilled, and the kingdom of God is at hand; repent, and believe in the gospel." (Mark 1:15)

Speaking by the authority of the Holy Spirit, St. Peter set forth Cross and Gospel as the one eternal truth and the one universal salvation: "Let all the house of Israel therefore know assuredly that God has made him both Lord and Christ, this Jesus whom you crucified . . . . And there is salvation in no one else, for there is no other name under heaven given among men by which we must be saved." (Act 2:36, 4:12)

Long before Christ's sacrificial death on the Cross, God's call for repentance and spiritual renewal went out through the prophet Habakkuk. But the summons to a life of faith also contained God's message of hope: "Behold, he whose soul is not upright in him shall fail, but the righteous shall live by his faith." (Habakkuk 2:4)

This very same life-giving truth of the Word of God was picked up by St. Paul. Christ's dedicated servant to Jews and Gentiles alike heralded God's eternal plan of salvation by grace through faith as the power of the Gospel: "For in it the righteousness of God is revealed through faith for faith; as it is written, 'He who through faith is righteous shall live.' " (Romans 1:17)

The Bible focuses on how people manipulate their spiritual similarity with God for personal gain. It exposes the sin caused by humanity's failure to use the power of God for establishing and advancing the Kingdom of God on earth. It declares the proper uses of God's power, the way God intended it to be used when divine power was made available as the great blessing for all human creation.

Christ told the Samaritan woman that "God is spirit, and those who worship him must worship in spirit and truth." (John 4:24) Renewed emphasis is directed toward spiritual oneness with God in preparation of a new type of covenant relationship between God and people. The center and cornerstone of this relationship is Jesus Christ. Its worldly manifestation is Cross and Gospel.

Through God's act of redemption in Jesus Christ, the Bible has suddenly changed from a lexicon of law to the encyclopedia of faith. In it we find information for spiritual growth. The lesson on truth starts with Abram, who "believed the LORD; and he reckoned it to him as righteousness." (Genesis 15:6)

Throughout the Bible's inspirational teaching, faith is presented within a covenant relationship of trust, justice, and love. Love is given priority as a mutual and reciprocal commitment of faithfulness between God and people. "For I desire steadfast love and not sacrifice, the knowledge of God, rather than burnt offerings." (Hosea 6:6)

This type of love is the direct result of true repentance, as God demanded through the prophet Amos: "Take away from me the noise of your songs; to the melody of your harps I will not listen. But let justice roll down like waters, and righteousness like an ever-flowing stream." (Amos 5:23-24)

As the literature of faith, the many "context stories" in the Bible require objective examination. Cultural background and living conditions are always unique to specific environments in time and place. What may have been readily obvious to people in Biblical times may be totally unknown in the present age.

Thus, proper comprehension of the Bible's content requires thorough study with a dedication that is typical of critical scholarship. But the prime factor in learning the truth about God is faith.

The necessary commitment for Bible study is different from any of the commitments that people must make in the world, if they want to succeed in what they are doing. Though the logistics may be similar, the concern for the Kingdom of God is above everything else we may think of in the world. The effort spent in sorting and weighing of the many variables in Biblical literature—of which time, place, and method of presentation are but a few—is then part of the investment for discipleship.

When under the guidance of the Holy Spirit grace and faith combine, then the Word of God as a divine message in the Bible becomes active and alive in the believer's heart. The written word, indeed, is human, but its inspirational message is divine.

As we look at the humanity of Biblical literature, we find, first of all, that the written word revolves around oral tradition for long periods of time. Secondly, composition and authorship is a matter of great scholarly debate.

For example, The Torah, or Pentateuch, is judged by many scholars to be the work of three, possibly four, literary traditions. The oldest of the documents may have originated about 1,000 years before Christ. Newer writings in the Hebrew canon may have been compiled around the fifth century B.C.

Yet independent of authorship and composition, Old Testament literature is credited as the single most impor-

tant factor in the survival of Judaism. And its contribution
to Christianity, and the quality of Western life per se, must
be acknowledged in praises and thanksgiving to Almighty
God.

Thus, all readers of Biblical literature should recognize
that of ultimate importance to human life is God's inspirational message through revelation by the Holy Spirit. Revelation alone makes the Word of God become active and
alive in people. The written word—whether executed by
hand as in ancient times or mass-produced by printing
machines—is but a vehicle, by means of which the Holy
Spirit makes known to faithful believers the truth about
God.

Eternal truth and universal salvation as the essence of
Christianity is God's message in Biblical literature. The
written word continues to preserve hope for all generations, because God's love for people is the eternal truth of
Cross and Gospel.

Biblical literature is a blessing from God to strengthen
and purify the faith, and the means by which the Holy
Spirit inspires people. Its narrative must not be misused.

For example, the Bible is not a weapon to enforce doctrine or a tool to manipulate behavior in people for getting a
certain response. The Bible does not relate to goal-oriented
psychology and its many schemes and mechanisms to control people by playing on their emotions.

The truth about God is not enhanced even by the most
noble of human intentions. Dedication to God must have
Christ as its foundation. Our faithfulness and obedience
alone will prove the pertinence of Biblical literature in the
affairs of daily life.

The world's best effort is not good enough when we mix
worldly ambitions with eternal truth, however sincere our
intentions may be in creating dogmas, developing theologi-

cal precepts, or even employing creative energies to speculate about the future. All human manipulation of the truth
about God is evil, for the pertinence of Biblical literature in
the affairs of daily life is a matter of revelation by the Holy
Spirit.

God has always made his will known for any specific
needs at hand. So let us live in faith and put the future in
God's hands. The relationship between God and people
requires faith, dedication, trust, but most of all love—love
for God and people around us.

8

God's Prophet Elijah and His Challenge

If our desire to overcome the current identity crisis is at all sincere, spiritual reawakening must become the order of the day. Good intentions alone never accomplish anything.

Newness of life and restored fellowship with God are based on God's righteousness. It is, therefore, important to thoroughly comprehend Old Testament writings.

Biblical stories are a distinct part of our Christian heritage. But Old Testament literature must be read and understood in terms of Cross and Gospel. The revealed meaning of these writings completes the total presentation of the truth about God.

We must recognize God's sacrifice on the Cross as the fulfillment of Law and Prophets. Christ's teaching confirmed this eternal truth. And through God's action on the Cross, we can now experience salvation by grace through faith.

This gift has its firm foundation established on the righteousness of God. Its reality in daily life is demonstrated through an intimate working relationship with the living God. Christianity details this opportunity from God for spiritually enslaved people to become free again through a life of union with Christ. Christ says, "If you continue in my word, you are truly my disciples, and you will know the truth, and the truth will make you free." (John 8:31-32)

However, as a free people of God, we can choose the quality of our life. We have the option, for example, to seek or reject God's purpose for our life. We also have the freedom to receive God's blessing in Biblical literature as a matter of faith. Or, we can study the Word of God judiciously from a strictly intellectual point of view, where critical scholarship is like an investigative tool.

Each approach has its own merits. But only when we commit ourselves to learn the truth about God with a dedication that demands faith will we benefit from God's blessing when reading the Bible.

The function of theology is to help faith appreciate what God through Christ has done.

God has demonstrated divine power in action for billions of years. Specifically we are forced to admit perfection in the movement of the planet Earth within the constellation of the heavenly bodies for over four-and-one-half billion years. New discoveries of scientifically documented facts serve as additional evidence that even the smallest particle is pertinent to the perfect motion of the universe.

With this knowledge, we have no choice but to suddenly feel humbled. Humility compels us to acknowledge our privileged status as redeemed people of God. We are blessed to know, worship, and serve the Almighty God of Creation, who, in His wisdom, also saw to it that every part of the human body is functional and unique.

Let there be no doubt, the eternal power of God is truly visible in the exactness that sustains the performance of the universe as well as in the perfection of grace that provides care for human beings on earth. The supplement of grace to the miraculous space-time continuum is beyond all descriptive language, even the words of Babylonian mythology. It requires faith to experience God in personal life and see God in all that exists. We must yield to eternal truth.

There is no theology in existence that can fathom God's eternal power. Nor are there adequate words in any language to fully describe the divine will that Christians know and witness to as the grace of God in Cross and Gospel.

Thus, full appreciation and revealed understanding of eternal truth and universal salvation is a matter of faith. All meaningful relationships with the living God are a matter of faith and dedication.

So we find that within this context of a faith relationship—though in the setting of the legalistic covenant—the prophet Elijah confronted Israelites in the Northern Kingdom: "How long will you go limping with two different opinions? If the LORD is God, follow him; but if Baal, then follow him." (1 Kings 18:21)

Let us explore some of the background leading up to this encounter. About 1200 years before Elijah's challenge, the covenant of faith and promise with Abraham was the means by which God had chosen to make Himself known. God's offer to relate to people on earth was consummated when Abraham "believed the LORD; and he reckoned it to him as righteousness." (Genesis 15:6) Abraham had responded to God's expectation by giving up his old identity. Because of it, he subsequently found perfection through his new relationship to God. Abraham lived in God's presence.

As time went on divine promise was fulfilled some 400 years later when on Mount Sinai God declared a covenant with Abraham's progeny.

A nation was born!

All the reasons for everlasting celebration were contained in God's covenant that crowned Israel's miraculous rescue from bondage and slavery in Egypt. Though the conditions for sharing God's blessings were clearly defined, pride and outright rejection immediately separated God and people. The evil in human nature surfaced on so many

occasions that God punished the evil generation of the
newly formed nation by denying them the blessing of the
promised land.

The historian of Deuteronomy framed the rocky start of
Judaism in the words of God's unforgettable challenge. In it
blessing and curse are equated to life and death: "I call
heaven and earth to witness against you this day, that I
have set before you life and death, blessing and curse;
therefore choose life, that you and your descendants may
live, loving the LORD your God, obeying his voice, and
cleaving to him; for that means life to you and length of
days . . . ." (Deuteronomy 30:19-20)

Life on earth is a matter of priorities. This message was
explicitly given in Deuteronomy and again vociferously
proclaimed by Elijah on Mount Carmel: "If the LORD is
God, follow him; but if Baal, then follow him." (1 Kings
18:21)

The ultimate question as to "how long will you go limping with two different opinions?" (1 Kings 18:21) culmi-
nated the three years of drought that Elijah had previously
predicted. Starvation, physical as well as spiritual, produced the agony that set the stage for exposing apostasy in
Northern Israel.

The prearranged marriage between King Ahab and the
Tyrian princess Jezebel was but a minor detail in the long
events of rampant faithlessness in Northern Israel. The
marriage only served to magnify the ongoing problem of
rebellion against God.

Through heinous manipulation of power, Jezebel returned idol worship, specifically the worship of the Phoeni-
cian fertility god Baal, to the land that God had previously
destined for the Israelites because of the very fact that its
earlier inhabitants had lavished in idol worship. Jezebel's
vicious threats intimidated the residents of the urban cen-

ters. She had succeeded in imposing her version of Baal worship. Hindrances were solved by a very efficient process—which, unfortunately, has carried over into modern times in the form of character assassination. Jezebel was determined to destroy the Israelites' orthodox view of dependence on God. Death was the ultimate enforcer of her ambition.

But during the heat of conflict, God stood by His prophet. God answered Elijah's prayer for mercy on the people and the LORD sent fire down in approval of Elijah's sacrifice offering. The event on Mount Carmel was not intended to teach people conversion through fear, although this was precisely the result: "And when all the people saw it, they fell on their faces; and they said, 'The LORD, he is God; the LORD, he is God.' " (1 Kings 18:39)

God's eternal lesson through this incident on Mount Carmel was to expose the futility of idol worship. The language used by Elijah to lead on the prophets of Baal excels satire and comedy, especially because of its Biblical setting: "At noon Elijah mocked them, saying, 'Cry aloud, for he is a god; either he is musing, or he has gone aside, or he is on a journey, or perhaps he is asleep and must be awakened.' " (1 Kings 18:27)

Now about 800 years later, roughly 2000 years from the present time, the Elijah of Christianity was pointing to the Master we all must serve. John the Baptist opened the prelude to the Gospel. And Jesus Christ preached the Good News from God: "I have come in order that you might have life—life in all its fullness." (John 10:10)TEV

Christians have reason to bask in the promise of the resurrected Christ: "I am with you always, to the close of the age." (Matthew 28:20)

9

Family

As disciples of Christ we are all members of the family of faith. We claim restored fellowship with God through salvation by grace through Jesus Christ.

But within this large family, each unit is a sacred entity in itself. God has ordained the separate existence of human families so that individuals can strengthen each other for worship and service.

The sanctity of the family is an acknowledged fact among faithful believers. God has blessed its existence with the promise of posterity. In proof of this statement let us recall the teaching from the book of Genesis: "Therefore a man leaves his father and his mother and cleaves to his wife, and they become one flesh." (Genesis 2:24)

In further explanation of God's purpose concerning the family unit, Jesus speaks about divorce and adultery. These have been subjects of concern since the Law was given to Moses. They have a direct influence on the performance of family life. In these discussions, Christ cites the Scriptures to demonstrate their validity and truth.

Christ says, "Have you not read that he who made them from the beginning made them male and female, and said, 'For this reason a man shall leave his father and mother and be joined to his wife, and the two shall become one'? So they are no longer two but one. What therefore God has joined together, let no man put asunder." (Matthew 19:4-6)

St. Paul expands on Christ's teaching on the family as a unit set apart for God's purpose and service. His teaching implies that the family has a similar significance to the world as the Church does to Christ.

Love, which is paramount in Christ's church, is cited by Paul as the coherent agent that also holds the family together. St. Paul speaks further in terms of mutual respect and reciprocating concern: "Be subject to one another out of reverence for Christ." (Ephesians 5:21) These components are inherent in the rule of grace. God through Christ has chosen us for holiness, but our response in faith is necessary to put God's plan into action.

As God and people then work together for the advancement of the Kingdom of God on earth by means of the church, so does solid family life advance civilization on earth. The example of husband and wife is used by Paul in this demonstration (Ephesians 5:21-33). St. Paul's theme is analogous to the teaching in the Gospel, where the church is identified as the bride of Christ. The bond of marriage is evidence of a strong church as well as a sign of vitality within a happy family.

We must, therefore, value and honor the family as an instrument of God. It has specific significance in mankind's journey on earth. God intended the family to be a haven of rest from the daily weariness of soul and body.

Within the family we give and receive physical support and emotional encouragement. Society also benefits because the stability of family life provides a sound basis for progress.

A stable home environment is also rewarding for personal advancement in faith. Spiritual growth is a building process that requires a sound foundation. Besides these benefits to individual life, the family also enhances a more meaningful continuation of civilization. Let there be no doubt, the family is an essential part in God's plan of creation. This has been made obvious through an over-abundance of God's blessing when Jesus Christ is the center of family life.

To be sure, Christ has singled out individuals who believe and do the will of God and called them his family (Matthew 12:50). But Christ also chose children—the very element that assures human posterity, and who are the fruit of love between husband and wife—as examples in the teachings about the Kingdom of God. We see God's message about humility (Matthew 18:4), temptations to sin (Matthew 18:6), and the availability of God's Kingdom (Matthew 19:14) brought to people by way of a child's experience.

These statements encourage us to be more assertive in our views about the family's contribution to the church. They beckon us to categorically affirm that the family of God flourishes because of people who practice at home what they publicly confess in church. The fruitful environment of a happy family life lends support to God's message of salvation. The home is the right place for the Gospel of Christ to mold the lives of young people. History is full of successful family participation in the growth of Christ's church ever since its formation at Jerusalem.

The worshiping family translates divine force into work. The power within families is so immense that mountainous obstacles vanish before it. Its power is only diminished when worldly ambitions sever the tie of restored fellowship with God. Then the family unit disintegrates because of the resultant disharmony and hate.

The family that is "made in heaven," to borrow the cliche of the world, is ordained by God. It knows its responsibility to God as its first and most important requirement for existence. Such a family then works harmoniously to fulfill its responsibility.

This is the only way that the purpose of God can be

fulfilled for perpetuating faith and civilization. Within such a framework, selfish ambitions are submerged.

Our foremost concern is the happiness and well-being of the other person simply because we want to share our abundance of God's blessing. We do it joyfully, for we ourselves feel secured in Christ. We know that we are well taken care of.

It is quite plausible to say that this is nothing but talk. It sounds good. But such a state is only utopia. It cannot be achieved in real-life situations. Human nature is contrary to all that is "good and nice."

The problem really is the evil of human nature. Therefore, let us control human nature so that it has no influence over the family of God. The Word of God, and the teaching of Christ, is sufficient to sustain believers in Christ's model of the godly life.

The world that is totally absorbed by human nature does not know Christ, nor his teaching, nor the model of the godly life. The world is not interested to hear that God expects of it faithfulness and obedience. The world has its own doctrines and teachings.

Because the unbelieving world rejects the Word of God, it will never have an active part in it. Nor will it know the peace that it provides for all believers. Thus, the family in the world outside the will of God is in real trouble.

The family of believers is the Church of Christ. This truth was singled out by Christ when identifying eternal relationships: "My mother and my brothers are those who hear the word of God and do it." (Luke 8:21) Consequently, it must act as light for the world and reflect the glory of God through Christ, who is the family's own beacon unto life eternal. The life of the Christian family is like a relay lens. It receives and then magnifies the glory of God. This kind of response substantiates the words of Christ: "Let your light so shine before men, that they may see your good works and give glory to your Father who is in heaven." (Matthew 5:16)

The world that refuses to receive Christ is totally ignorant of grace and salvation. Because of this very ignorance, people in the world call the life in the Spirit utopia.

Because the world does not know Christ, neither will it then understand matters concerning the Spirit. The world's only interest is in shortsighted goals and objectives. Therefore, it has set up institutions that are supposedly highly efficient. But, in reality, these organizations are many times ineffective, even by the world's own evaluation and standards.

Any shortcomings are explained away. In worst-case conditions, they are covered up and lied about. Yet we find people in these worldly institutions exerting pressure on the family life of others.

Administrators of government programs dealing with family structure and coherence work according to legislated objectives. There is no freedom of choice in the working of the law, even though some family discords before social agencies warrant a less rigid treatment.

This is especially true where family problems fall within "gray areas," where either circumstances or law are not clearly defined. What a strong family could remedy with a simple reprimand when one of its members strays becomes a "case" for the social worker. For instance, young people, who are still in the formative stages of their lives, are drawn into the system of government machinery, where there are no provisions for emotional support to sustain a second chance. Past behavior and future guidance become fixed as a matter of record, even though the opportunity of a new beginning—so essential to the correction of social attitudes and behavioral patterns—should be flexible enough to accommodate specific needs. This is found within healthy families who work the principle of love.

The formality of government proceedings alone brands a person for life, and a marginal situation can become hopeless. Let us consider the story of Karl, a spirited 16-year-old, whose young life had always bordered on chaos because the family environment was predictably unstable. He was unwanted by his stepfather and unwittingly rejected by his mother because she felt her new family threatened because of him. There was no place for Karl in the "new home." In a moment of foolishness, Karl was reckless and had destroyed property.

His "family" formally rejected him as a stubborn and destructive child, and he was temporarily put in a correctional institution. At the time of his commitment, no provisions were made for Karl's future or guardianship; his mother retained control.

After serving his debt to society, Karl was released with a commendation for his model behavior. He returned to his town, but he really had no place to go. He dared not enter the family home. He opted for shelter in the barn of a nearby estate, lit a cigarette and fell asleep. Exploding flames burned the place to the ground and with it also went all hope for a better future. His life was saved. But society now looked at him as a criminal.

Karl was held responsible for illegal entry and setting a fire, while those involved in his predicament leading up to this ordeal were absolved from all blame. People reasoned that it is impossible to predict what kids will do. "This fellow 'should have' known better; he deserved what was coming to him." Many children, like Karl, are victims of family discord and bureaucracy. They are never given a chance to work out the purpose of their being.

Therefore, let us recall the teaching of Christ and check

our involvement in raising children: "Whoever receives one such child in my name receives me; but whoever causes one of these little ones who believe in me to sin, it would be better for him to have a great millstone fastened round his neck and to be drowned in the depth of the sea." (Matthew 18:5-6)

Severity of punishment for our failure to comply is implied in Christ's strong words of exhortation: "Woe to the world for temptation to sin! For it is necessary that temptations come, but woe to the man by whom the temptations come." (Matthew 18:7)

But the family that follows the model of the godly life has Christ as its center. This family will withstand pressure and influence that could harm its relationship with God. It will survive despite the fact that worldly institutions are embroiled in its affairs and seemingly even wield power that dictates their authority over it.

And the family dedicated to God recognizes its obligation to draw on His power because it wants to do the will of God. When we see this happening, then Christianity is the living faith that God had ordained it to be.

When the purpose of God is fulfilled, the family then has rightfully assumed its core position within the Church of Christ. And Christ, as the Lord of His Church, will supply all of God's blessings so that it can properly and successfully reach out with the message of salvation that is the Good News of the Gospel of Christ.

Divisions in the family will be healed only when we prayerfully request God's intervention and prepare ourselves in a way so that God can act. God is the source of all power, as by God's power the family unit was created and sanctified.

Therefore, God alone is the power who can restore it when the difficulties of trials and temptations are overtaxing the family's ability to handle them. Because God established and ordained the family, we can rest assured that God will also sustain it through times of trouble.

Thus, the healing process of the family unit is a matter of divine power AND our faith. But we must remember that God's healing process demands our commitment before it can start. The family that was created by God can only be healed and restored by God through Christ when a genuine effort is made to rebuild what was torn down and to mend what had been ripped apart.

This genuine effort is evident when contrite hearts seek forgiveness from God and through Christ seek forgiveness from one another. When this happens, then the Holy Spirit of God takes over as the mentor. And we suddenly will experience the Spirit's work as the Helper that Christ has provided for comfort and as guide in our short pilgrimage on earth. The Holy Spirit supports our life on earth.

It is not uncommon to find the family, which is the unit that God has ordained as His instrument for posterity, to be under constant attack from within as well as by Satan's external forces. Any family that is forced to live under internal duress becomes drained of its energy. It will have little strength left to withstand long periods of attacks, unless it seeks the power of God and prepares itself for reconciliation if it is to survive.

If this is not done, then it will succumb to the forces of discord, and envy and greed are substituted for the genuine love that the family members once shared with one another.

Signs of discord are evident when we fail to respect the feelings of our spouses and neglect each other's needs; or when we fail to take seriously our obligation in raising children.

The story of Bill and Sue exemplify this point. Like

people in Christ's parable of the Sower (Luke 8:11-15), they also enjoyed the temporary bliss of something new. Both were full of stary-eyed admiration for each other during the festivities of their wedding ceremony. Their honeymoon to the Caribbean was equally rewarding. It was like a visit to paradise. They found all the trimmings in proper place: sandy beaches, blue sky, gentle breezes and, most importantly, the companionship of people in love.

They were happy with each other. Bill was a clever engineer and overflowing with confidence. He found satisfaction at work and enjoyed life at home. The dream house became complete with two beautiful children.

But difficulties in their relationship surfaced when Bill's interests became self-centered; because of it the husband-wife communication started to fall apart. Sue was talking about Brownies and Boy Scouts. She recited the children's adventure stories for she knew them so well. And she also talked about helping them unlock doors when they got stuck with problems and homework. Bill used "equal time" to bore the family with shop language. His one-way conversation analyzed his expertise with computers, his acumen for business, and he also bragged about the future and growth of the family's investments. Sue could care less. And to the children, these were fairy tales.

Sue was frustrated because of the lack of coherence within the family. And Bill harbored hurt feelings because no one really paid any attention.

Short moments of deadly silence started to grow longer as mealtimes actually shortened. Only Sue's love and energy held the family together; Bill never wasted time in keeping current on bank balances, money market certificates, and stocks. A once happy family was courting disaster.

This was prevented from happening by a moment of

truth, which confronted Bill and Sue with the demand of
faithfulness and obedience to God. This came by means of a
phone call from their mutual friend Jim. He was desperate
and in need of money. He had been out of work for some
time, his health insurance had lapsed, and now Bill's and
Sue's godson Scott needed surgery. Could they help?

No time was wasted; they helped. By giving of themselves they again found each other in the need of another
person. Perhaps Bill's sudden embrace of Sue was sparked
by God's love for a struggling human family. We can only
speculate, but God knows.

A strong family is like a healthy tree. When its roots are
soundly anchored in fertile soil, this tree will draw from
God's fountain all the nutrients that it will ever need for
growth.

As individual branches draw on the central supply and
leaves then display the sheen that indicates a healthy root
system, so it is with the family when it builds its foundation
on the Word of God.

The Christian family radiates happiness and peace as a
shining light. Its intensity penetrates darkness. The Christian family knows that its light is shining bright because its
source of energy is the powerful Word of God.

Therefore, it reflects the stability of a system that is
secured in the righteousness of God, the only source from
which life-sustaining energy must be drawn. The stability
of life, individual and family, truly comes from God
through Christ, as Christ is both cornerstone and foundation of a secure and peaceful family life.

So that we fully understand our obligation and fulfill
God's purpose in living as a family of God, we must put in
proper perspective our relationship with one another and
with God. Our examination must begin with the purpose of
our creation.

We must correctly answer the question whose we truly are. The answer to this crucial question will reveal that the family is the most significant element in the fellowship of believers. The Christian family in a growing civilization then fulfills the purpose of giving praise, glory, and honor to God.

The family is the instrument of God. It must be keen on all matters concerning the Word of God. This is what the Holy Spirit will reveal to each family member individually when Jesus Christ is the center of family life.

Christ explained to the disciples that his death on the Cross and our sharing in his resurrection will make possible the Spirit's work among us: "I tell you the truth: it is to your advantage that I go away, for if I do not go away, the Counselor will not come to you; but if I go, I will send him to you." (John 16:7) Therefore, Christ says: "When the Spirit of truth comes, he will guide you into all the truth; for he will not speak on his own authority, but whatever he hears he will speak, and he will declare to you the things that are to come. He will glorify me, for he will take what is mine and declare it to you." (John 16:13-14)

The Christian family then will have more than sufficient strength to overcome trials and temptations. It knows security from its trust in God and expresses this trust in the belief that it exists by the grace of God only. It knows that the power of God is in this grace and through this grace it knows how to share the love of God.

It knows that the divine love that promised salvation and decreed redemption is at work within the family and unites it through love for one another. This type of family we find fully dedicated to God in faithful and obedient service. Its existence is the truth of the new life in the Spirit.

It is certain that the Christian family wields power—the power of love, which itself is being received by it as the constant outpouring of God's abundant blessing. This Christian family knows God. Christ is in its midst.

Through this connection, the Christian family knows God's reservoir of wealth and it is neither afraid nor ashamed to make use of it, as we indeed must if we are faithful to God and obedient to His will that commands us to reach out to all of God's people. Only then do we fulfill our mission as the beacon that radiates God's glory.

The Christian family knows laughter, because it shares the joy of the new life in the Spirit. It knows how to laugh at itself because it knows the true security that comes from being a disciple of Christ.

The medicine of happiness that is produced by a soul that is securely rested in Christ has greater healing power for body and mind than any artificial formulations. Laughter is medicine. It is the contentment that comes from the knowledge that our lives are sustained by the grace of God.

The Holy Spirit keeps the Christian family in a state of constant blessing by revealing to it the truth about God. The truth in God's Word alone is the power that sustains the family until Christ comes and takes each individual family member unto Himself. The security of the family is based on a complete trust in God. The basis for this trust is God's grace. The tool for implementing it is faith.

Material riches do not indicate either true wealth or security of any family. This was shown to us by Christ in the Parable of the Rich Fool. Christ's directive comes as a warning: "Take heed, and beware of all covetousness; for a man's life does not consist in the abundance of his possessions." (Luke 12:15)

In continuation of Christ's teaching, St. Paul instructs believers to place proper attention on their relationship with God. We must not let the world overtake us. Wealth gives apparent power. But this power is never real, because what God has designated as a vehicle has been wrongfully turned into an authority. St. Paul writes to Timothy:

"For the love of money is the root of all evils; it is through this craving that some have wandered away from the faith and pierced their hearts with many pangs. But as for you, man of God, shun all this; aim at righteousness, godliness, faith, love, steadfastness, gentleness. Fight the good fight of the faith; take hold of the eternal life to which you were called when you made the good confession in the presence of many witnesses. In the presence of God who gives life to all things, and of Christ Jesus who in his testimony before Pontius Pilate made the good confession, I charge you to keep the commandment unstained and free from reproach until the appearing of our Lord Jesus Christ; and this will be made manifest at the proper time by the blessed and only Sovereign, the King of kings and the Lord of lords, who alone has immortality and dwells in unapproachable light, whom no man has ever seen or can see. To him be honor and eternal dominion. Amen." (1 Timothy 6:10-16)

10

Family and Work

1. Assessment of Everyday Situations

The relationship of family and work deals with all aspects of human behavior. It will require a lot of effort on our part to make this relationship successful and smooth running. Our attitudes and views on life are very important elements for establishing the necessary stability that will help us to function properly at home and at work.

Even though we must strive to separate home and work, we find that this division is not easily achieved. Unresolved issues at home usually spill over into our work life. In like manner, unfinished business is carried home.

So we find it very difficult to suddenly empty our minds from every burden of a tough day. There are always some remaining pressures within us.

But only when we are not preoccupied with other problems can we give our full attention to the matters at hand, whether at home or at work. Yet we must be fully aware of the interrelation of family and work. Our encounters in either have definite bearings on the other.

Happiness at home has an influence on our work performance. And we also know the robust impact that our job income has on our family. Our action and reaction in either situation contributes to the groundwork for building a well-rounded stability in the human family. This stability also implies that we dedicate our lives to discipleship in Christ.

Emotions have a significant influence on stability. But emotions are cyclical. We are not machines that can be turned on or off simply by the throw of a switch.

The only way that our emotions can be controlled is through total submission to Christ and by letting him be the master of our lives. Only then can we realize the joy of family life and receive satisfaction from doing our work. We will then also be in harmony with the objectives of God for our lives. This realization is but another form of blessing that we constantly receive from God.

We have plenty of reasons for not letting God be God. We are too stubborn to let our Creator work His will and purpose through us. In support of this stubbornness, we then build our defense through false belief systems. Abilities and strengths join forces with pride and complicate matters further through the whispering of self-assurance. This then prevents people from realizing that we have wandered from the narrow path prescribed by God.

In other words, we have chosen to forsake the secure environment provided by God for our temporary journey on earth, and we have sinfully created an existence outside the protective custody of God.

Even today we continue to fall into the trap of personal ambition despite the numerous accounts in history that tell us over and over again that the cost of this rebellion toward God is very high. The Word of God tells us that whoever falls into this trap is subject to condemnation, misery, despair, and ultimate death.

Our destiny then becomes sealed, because we rejected the grace of God, which could have led us into the presence of God and eternal life.

We are neither the first nor are we alone in this rebellion against the purpose of our creation. For example, we see the Psalmist bemoaning the sins of past generations as he cites the rebellious behavior of the Israelites in their life's journey.

The descriptive account of their travel through the desert to the promised land is symbolic of our soul's pilgrimage on earth. Like the Israelites, we are also quick to forget whose we truly are. Like them, we also are very eager to declare ourselves masters of our own destiny: "But they soon forgot his works; they did not wait for his counsel." (Psalms 106:13)

Because we also have rejected the evidence of what God has done for mankind and continue to act and "not wait for his counsel," we are guilty of not trusting God. Because of this unbelief, we lose our usefulness to God. Instead of searching for truth, we become preoccupied with ourselves. Thus, we are looking for trouble as "the cares of the world and the delight in riches choke the word, and it proves unfruitful." (Matthew 13:22)

These words of Christ taken from the explanation of the Parable of the Sower (Matthew 13:18-23) illustrate what happens when the Word of God reaches people that have no faith.

Whenever people choose to live without faith, they do not believe that God will do all that He has promised. And we fail to wait for God's directions. As a result, we gradually drift away from God's presence and let family and work turn into unbearable burdens instead of developing them into the blessings that God had commanded us to do.

Therefore, since we have fallen short of our commitment to God and not properly fulfilled our responsibility because of personal excursions to explore self, we must treat the interrelation of family and work as a subject of grave importance. Through it we channel the results of our behavior from this world into eternity.

2. *Spiritual Blindness*

Difficulties within some families can spill into other family units when poor attitudes toward job performance and lack of cooperation among workers affects the place of employment. Companies are in business to make money. People must work to earn a living. Any mismatch will prove chaotic to either side.

Cooperation and respect at the workplace may not always be mutual. This usually is also the case in family situations. It is proven that relationships thrive best when respect, feelings, and understanding are reciprocal.

Family life gives us an opportunity to practice our faith at home. We need not make a search to determine who our neighbor is when we are confronted with the needs of members in our own family.

But our human nature is at times vehemently opposed to helping our own flesh and blood. Instead, we prefer to go out of our way trying to find strangers that we are more ready and willing to help whether or not they really need it.

This peculiar characteristic is a curse in human nature that makes us shy away from helping those we should truly love. We misuse the grace of God and make it selective.

There is no doubt we are spiritually blinded whenever we behave in this manner. God is being shoved out of our lives when we put our ideas in the forefront as to how people should live, especially the poor and distressed. People are more willing to judge than to help. But God's gift to mankind for living peaceably with each other is captured in our tolerance, compassion, and mercy.

Christ's parable about the Good Samaritan (Luke 10:25-37) is a good example.

God commands that we work to bring glory to Him (Matthew 5:16). This also applies to the workplace, where we have the opportunity to ask whether we are helping or hindering those who are not quite as quick in doing their job as we are. The workplace is God's laboratory for developing team effort in demonstration of successful balance of different talents. A floor sweeper whose concern is to do the best possible job is a better person than the gifted loudmouth who neglects craftsmanship.

Abilities and talents are our tools for doing this. Another vivid example of being helpful are words of encouragement to young people who are tense when learning a new job. The workplace has unlimited opportunities to transform prejudice and intolerance into leadership.

Therefore, let us not shy away from those who need support. We must become aware that we are part of God's solution to problems and handicaps—within ourselves and those around us.

Christ explained spiritual blindness in giving sight to the man born blind. In this miracle, Christ demonstrated the mighty power of God at work: "For judgment I came into this world, that those who do not see may see, and that those who see may become blind." (John 9:39)

We are thereby told that we must envision the work of God with the humble eyes of our soul and let the Holy Spirit of God reveal it to our spirit. We will never perceive the work of God in the arrogance of the flesh. It is only by the power of the Spirit of God living in us that we will ever be able to exercise the power of God while living in the flesh. Only then can we recognize God's work as bringing light—that is truth—into the world. Our light, therefore, must "shine before men, that they may see your good

works and give glory to your Father who is in heaven."
(Matthew 5:16)

Christ implies that the power of God is light. It dispels
the darkness of evil as embodied in disbelief. Therefore,
Christ says, "We must work the works of him who sent me,
while it is day; night comes, when no one can work. As long
as I am in the world, I am the light of the world." (John
9:4-5)

3. Priorities

The importance of the interrelation of family and work
must not become neglected. We spend a significant
amount of time and a good portion of our energy in these
domains.

In our selection of priorities, whether at home or at
work, we exercise the choice to either serve God or reject
His authority over our lives.

But whatever choice is made will definitely determine
our ultimate destiny. Therefore, let us beware! If our inten-
tion is to excel through the merits of good works, we have
already fallen into the trap of works righteousness. But only
faith can secure God's blessing of eternal life. The judgment of God is rendered depending upon the priorities of
our life on earth.

The opportunity to choose is ours. But so is also the
burden of our decision. Our rejection of God will definitely
consume us. Only our confession as disciples of Christ will
enhance our life in the Spirit for all eternity, for we will
have been true to the Word of God and have picked up our
cross and followed Christ.

Christ established our relationship with God and with
one another by directing us: "You shall love the Lord your

God with all your heart, and with all your soul, and with all your mind." (Matthew 22:37)

Likewise Jesus commands: "You shall love your neighbor as yourself." (Matthew 22:39)

Christ reminds us of our great efficiency in selfishness, greed, and lust for power and tells us to love our neighbor, and our family, with that very same efficiency! Our relationship with God and also with one another must become one of total involvement.

The first step in this total involvement is constantly praying for guidance from God's Holy Spirit. In His example of the godly life, Jesus drew life and strength from God the Father through prayer. Christ was showing us the way to the power of God. Let us pose for a moment and examine the question whether a servant can live differently from the life style of the master and still claim that he follows the master in obedient service.

The answer to this question is David's prayer for guidance and protection: "Make me to know thy ways, O LORD; teach me thy paths. Lead me in thy truth, and teach me, for thou art the God of my salvation; for thee I wait all the day long." (Psalms 25:4-5)

David's prayer expresses his heart's desire for steadfastness in commitment.

"Give me understanding," the Psalmist says, "that I may keep thy law and observe it with my whole heart." (Psalms 119:34)

We are shown by this example the model and the true meaning of allegiance.

In our restored fellowship with God there are no provisions for us to sway back and forth like a blade of grass bending in the wind. In our new life in the Spirit, we accept the Word of God as the authority over our lives. This we learn also by revelation of the Holy Spirit as the

Word of God becomes "a lamp to guide me and a light for my path." (Psalms 119:105)TEV

Therefore, our life in service to God is a matter of faithfulness and obedience. The opportunity is given by God, but the response of commitment is faith and wholehearted involvement: "I have laid up thy word in my heart, that I might not sin against thee." (Psalms 119:11)

Thus, we cannot be many things to different people, if our confession of discipleship in Jesus Christ is true and we consequently long to live the model of the godly life that Jesus Christ has demonstrated to us. If our confession and our commitment are sincere, then the only witness needed to confirm whether or not we are what we profess to be is our life itself.

Our life in Christ then is a matter of commitment, similar to the commitment that God had expected from the Israelites when He called on them to accept the conditions for restoration and blessing: "I call heaven and earth to witness against you this day, that I have set before you life and death, blessing and curse; therefore choose life, that you and your descendants may live, loving the LORD your God, obeying his voice, and cleaving to him; for that means life to you and length of days. . . ." (Deuteronomy 30:19-20)

4. Goals in life

We have gone through this discussion of commitment, faithfulness, and obedience at length to show that all successful relationships demand singlemindedness in purpose to reach the goal. The setting of the goal requires a commitment itself.

Any relationship will disintegrate if there is no unity in spirit. Good intentions do not make a relationship. But commitment does. And our dedication to this commitment makes relationships prosper and grow, as we put our interest into it to give it the necessary impetus for advancement.

We must work hard at relationships to make them work. Good intentions have no power and are not worth the breath of speech or the paper for recording.

Relationships succeed when promise and anticipation are matched by performance. To amplify this point, let us borrow an example from business. When negotiations are over and an order is received there is happiness over it but not yet satisfaction. Only after the delivery is made, can the supplier claim to have gained a satisfied customer. Business transactions are completed deals. We cannot enter promises and hopes on a profit-and-loss ledger.

Human nature is dualistic. This is shown in several conflicts we face in life:
—spiritual being versus physical nature
—immortality of the spirit versus mortality of the flesh
—obedience and faithfulness versus rejection of God.

These have been the plague of mankind since the days of the first sin of Adam and humanity's downfall and disgrace because of it.

This dualism expands into the realm of the cosmos, as we speak of the power of light and the power of darkness; the Kingdom of God—where grace creates and sustains life—and the world, where in the ideal democratic society government rules by justice for the purpose of order.

As human beings we are touched by this structure of good and evil. And we must choose in full knowledge that our choice will determine life or death. This conflict is bemoaned by St. Paul. But Paul also preaches the solution: "I do not understand my own actions. For I do not do what I want, but I do the very thing I hate . . . Wretched man that I am! Who will deliver me from this body of death?

Thanks be to God through Jesus Christ our Lord! So then, I of myself serve the law of God with my mind, but with my flesh I serve the law of sin." (Romans 7:15, 24-25)

The interrelation of family and work takes on significance in the world as society places certain values on our performance in family relationship and achievement at work. This judgment by peers can be cruel at times, because on many occasions we find conclusions reached that are not entirely based on fact.

In other instances we find opinions formed without any appreciation of circumstances. Our human nature has great talent to condemn and ostracize. When we are wrong, we do not wish to be reminded that we have erred.

We often say that it takes a real man—i.e. a strong person—to apologize for a mistake. But more is at stake when feelings and integrity are injured. Many people have left behind a growing cancer. The healing words, "I am sorry," or "I forgive you" were never spoken.

As disciples of Christ, we must not lower ourselves in dignity by responding to, or even acknowledging, any false accusations. Christ will in due time speak through the Spirit on our behalf and keep us safe from the Evil One.

Let us remember that we are not alone, even though the entire world may seem to be against us. Eternal life in the Spirit is more valuable than the temporary rectification of problems in a sinful world. We know the truth of the Word of God and through this truth we claim our freedom from any vile accusations. We can definitely afford to lose our life in the world.

Christ addresses this subject when speaking about His suffering and death: "For what will it profit a man, if he gains the whole world and forfeits his life? Or what shall a man give in return for his life?" (Matthew 16:26)

The price of humanity's salvation is Christ's suffering and

death. The world may never know this, but Christians do (1
Corinthians 1:18-31). And we have become instruments of
God's promise to advance the Kingdom of God on earth.
Our concern is Christ's work to bring God's message of
salvation to all people—even to those who may have of-
fended us.

God valued our life by reaching down into the pit of His
adulterated creation and lifting us out of it. So let us make it
our task to work on behalf of the Kingdom of God bringing
to the people in the world the message of salvation that we
ourselves have received as the Good News of the Gospel of
Christ. In this light, then, our sacrifice is God's work, as
the work of God is divine sacrifice that saves sinners.

Our concern for the other person overshadows the temporary loss of time we suffer because we do not look after
ourselves. God will bless the person who through our work
was brought to Christ. We automatically will share in this
blessing, as we are all one in Christ. We are merely draw-
ing on what God through Jesus Christ is providing.

5. At the Crossroads of Life

The true meaning for all our interrelations is found in
Jesus Christ, the living Word of God. The power of the
Word of God is the message of life that yields fruit of faith
for life eternal.

God used the words of promise for sealing the covenant
with the Israelites. He called on them to be faithful and
obedient: "Now therefore, if you will obey my voice and
keep my covenant, you shall be my own possession among
all peoples; for all the earth is mine, and you shall be to me
a kingdom of priests and a holy nation." (Exodus 19:5-6)

If the people's response of faithfulness and obedience
and their acceptance of God's promise made the Israelites

priests and servants, then how much more must we, as his disciples, serve Christ because "He saved us, not because of deeds done by us in righteousness, but in virtue of his own mercy, by the washing of regeneration and renewal in the Holy Spirit, which he poured out upon us richly through Jesus Christ our Savior, so that we might be justified by his grace and become heirs in hope of eternal life." (Titus 3:5-7)

Let us remember that our life in Jesus Christ is the fulfillment of God's promise. Christ "gave himself for us to redeem us from all iniquity and to purify for himself a people of his own who are zealous for good deeds." (Titus 2:14)

How, then, do we react to the gift of God?

Solomon's words of wisdom establish the boundary condition for our behavior. Let their truth refresh the weary mind and guide the tired soul in mapping a treacherous journey: "Unless the LORD builds the house, those who build it labor in vain. Unless the LORD watches over the city, the watchman stays awake in vain. It is in vain that you rise up early and go late to rest, eating the bread of anxious toil; for he gives to his beloved sleep." (Psalms 127:1-2)

So let us seriously look at relationships with God and also with one another. Equally important is to examine our attitude toward the work of God for which we were created. If we proceed according to God's plan, then our labor will be productive because it was done in light of fulfilling the expectation of God.

We respond to God in love, because He first loved us. Our salvation through Jesus Christ is based on grace, that unmerited love of God for all humanity.

Our relationship with other people, as well as the interfacing of people and work, must reflect God's expectation and make our life a hymn of constant thanksgiving. The

Psalmist rejoices as he sings praises to God: "O give thanks to the LORD, for he is good; for his steadfast love endures for ever!" (Psalms 107:1)

We perceive the eternal goodness of God with the eyes of our soul. Our response is that kind of appreciation which prompts us to prepare in our heart a dwelling place for the Holy Spirit. Since a relationship of love involves the whole person, our dedication of love to God and our neighbor is total commitment.

True love cannot be acquired through analysis. Nor can it be created through study. Love requires a commitment of our total being.

It has its origin in understanding whose we are. It is instrumental in helping believers fulfill their mission of life on earth.

Human life draws its meaning from the Spirit. God has ordained equality for all people through this spiritual connection. This divine truth prevails despite the privileged claims of people arising from status and position in life.

Diversity because of status or achievement is real in the world. God has given each person different talents. Yet, let us all remember that these gifts come from the same Spirit. In the sight of God, this is complementary and not at all a discrepancy to be looked at with scorn.

St. Paul explains: "Now there are varieties of gifts, but the same Spirit; and there are varieties of service, but the same Lord; and there are varieties of working, but it is the same God who inspires them all in every one. To each is given the manifestation of the Spirit for the common good." (1 Corinthians 12:4-7)

We are part of God's team as we work in faith with our brothers and sisters in Christ to bring glory to God. The restored fellowship of all believers is God's answer to waywardness and sin.

Our equality before God is crowned by the divine act of grace. God made a sacrifice on behalf of sinners. Jesus Christ died for the forgiveness of all our sins. The word "all" extends to people everywhere. St. John clearly states this fact in the opening words of his Gospel, when he talks about John the Baptist being the messenger who "came for testimony, to bear witness to the light, that all might believe through him." (John 1:6)

6. *Divine Truth Versus Human Ambition*

We may blame our bad behavior on human nature. People are prone to defend any poor attitude toward life by saying that this is so because human nature is bad and makes it so.

This is not true!

When St. Paul speaks about the conflict in people, he does not point the accusing finger at all aspects of human nature, but at the sin in human nature. God has given us human nature, but we are responsible for its sin, the throne of which we have built in our mind. And its evil empire we sustain within our hearts through lusts and greed.

These are manifestations of selfishness. They have grown out of our disobedience and faithlessness toward God. St. Paul faced a similar problem. But he also says that we must properly recognize this as sin: "For I do not do the good I want, but the evil I do not want is what I do. Now if I do what I do not want, it is no longer I that do it, but sin which dwells within me." (Romans 7:19-20)

Let us now look more closely at the nature of our human character and trace it back to creation, and then examine God's response to our wayward behavior. We will soon learn that we are not really as great as we think we are. The Psalmist has recorded the truth of the Word of God:

"Hear, O my people, while I admonish you! O Israel, if you would but listen to me! There shall be no strange god among you; you shall not bow down to a foreign god.

"I am the Lord your God, who brought you up out of the land of Egypt. Open your mouth wide, and I will fill it.

"But my people did not listen to my voice; Israel would have none of me.

"So I gave them over to their stubborn hearts, to follow their own counsels.

"O that my people would listen to me, that Israel would walk in my ways!

"I would soon subdue their enemies, and turn my hand against their foes." (Psalms 81:8-14)

Only the Word of God can bridge the shortcoming created by the rebellion of people toward God. An outgrowth of our rejection of God is disrespect for human life. This evidence is commonly visible in dealing with less fortunate people and also those lower in status than ours. Such downgrading of people continues despite full knowledge that all humanity is God's creation. This perpetuation of the sin of discrimination is but a subtle form of an overall rebellion toward God.

The selection from the eighty-first Psalm discusses what human behavior is like. It also tells us what is being missed when people fall short of God's expectation of faithfulness and obedience.

God's address is a warning. But it definitely also contains the promise of hope. The Word of God assures us that when we worship God and with absolute reliance wait on Him for all our needs, then we will enjoy God's blessing of restored fellowship. To have this come about, we are firmly reminded of God's declaration from Exodus concerning the meaning of a true relationship: "You shall have no other gods before me." (Exodus 20:3)

Behind the authority of the address in this Psalm again is God's own power. The power of the Word of God already has been demonstrated in history. Here again are the specifics: "I am the LORD your God, who brought you out of the land of Egypt, out of the house of bondage." (Exodus 20:2) In detailed language, God is letting people know whose they are. He traces relationships for a clearer understanding. Believers now can be free of doubts.

The specificity of the Word of God, as recorded by the Psalmist, has been indeed fulfilled. We read the promise, "Open your mouth wide, and I will fill it." (Psalms 81:10b)

As disciples of Christ we suddenly feel overtaken as we realize the power of the Good News of the Gospel.

Christ took on human form for the sole purpose of saving sinners. Through God's act of grace, believers have the opportunity of receiving life and light. This is our redemption.

Jesus Christ dwelled among people. Christ is an event in human history: "In the beginning was the Word, and the Word was with God, and the Word was God. He was in the beginning with God; all things were made through him, and without him was not anything made that was made. In him was life, and the life was the light of men." (John 1:1-4)

As further evidence that the human race is really slow in learning, St. John writes that Christ was in the world as the light that ". . . enlightens every man . . . yet the world knew him not. He came to his own home, and his own people received him not." (John 1:9-11) Thus, people continue to live in disobedience toward God.

Consequently, we are given a foretaste of God's judgment: "So I gave them over to their stubborn hearts, to follow their own counsels." (Psalms 81:12)

When God abandons all intentions to discipline us further, let there not be any doubt that God's judgment is upon us.

St. Paul wrote to the members of the Church at Rome: "For the wrath of God is revealed from heaven against all ungodliness and wickedness of men who by their wickedness suppress the truth. For what can be known about God is plain to them, because God has shown it to them." (Romans 1:18-19)

Human resourcefulness, with all its excuses, is now exposed. Christ has affirmed: "As long as I am in the world, I am the light of the world." (John 9:5)

Despite anger and judgment, God's overwhelming concern for humanity is visible. Threads of mercy hold together a statement of compassion that is designed to inspire hope in people: "O that my people would listen to me, that Israel would walk in my ways!" (Psalms 81:13)

Jesus gives the Christian community the opportunity to follow Him as the light of the world. Christ has already paid the price for the forgiveness of sins. Now Christ illuminates this truth further. Salvation is a free gift from God: "I am the light of the world; he who follows me will not walk in darkness, but will have the light of life." (John 8:12)

To make sure that we grasp this fact of restored fellowship, we are told that the best way to show our new status as God's chosen people is by becoming what we continuously recite in the confessional creeds. Christ's reminder is additional help: "You are the light of the world . . . Let your light so shine before men, that they may see your good works and give glory to your Father who is in heaven." (Matthew 5:14,16)

Abraham was justified before God because of his trust in God's promise. How much more assurance then do we have in claiming our justification through God's act of righteousness, for which the death and the resurrection of Jesus Christ is the living example!

The desire to know truth transforms guilt into faith. Christ is there to help us cross the gulf of sin. As we recognize the Word of God, we will respect it as the only authority in our dealings during the soul's pilgrimage on earth. The value of the Word of God is secured for us in divine promise.

Believers are assured that the righteousness of God is all-sufficient, for even the worst of sinners, to find forgiveness and the return to God. All this has been made possible through Christ.

11

The Church

The Church of Christ revolves around one very important message: "Let all the house of Israel therefore know assuredly that God has made him both Lord and Christ, this Jesus whom you crucified . . . And there is salvation in no one else, for there is no other name under heaven given among men by which we must be saved." (Acts 2:36, 4:12)

With this message as its charter for existence, the Church of Christ then dedicates itself as a fellowship of believers to its only Lord, Jesus the Christ.

The church is the working tool of God's Holy Spirit. It is a collective representation of believers, who assemble for the purpose of unity in fellowship and service.

Christians take the message of the Gospel as an inspirational signal and then march forward in a mission of preaching and teaching. This community of believers makes up Christ's army of redeemed saints.

We have purposely chosen the qualified term "redeemed saints" to signify that our life on earth is still the combination of flesh and spirit. We have been redeemed by God through Jesus Christ, but we are not yet reconciled. In his writing on the subject of future glory, St. Paul says that believers must wait for it in hope: "For the creation waits with eager longing for the revealing of the sons of God; for the creation was subjected to futility, not of its own will but by the will of him who subjected it in hope;

because the creation itself will be set free from its bondage to decay and obtain the glorious liberty of the children of God. We know that the whole creation has been groaning in travail together until now; and not only the creation, but we ourselves, who have the first fruits of the Spirit, groan inwardly as we wait for adoption as sons, the redemption of our bodies. For in this hope we were saved. Now hope that is seen is not hope. For who hopes for what he sees? But if we hope for what we do not see, we wait for it with patience. Likewise the Spirit helps us in our weakness; for we do not know how to pray as we ought, but the Spirit himself intercedes for us with sighs too deep for words. And he who searches the hearts of men knows what is the mind of the Spirit, because the Spirit intercedes for the saints according to the will of God." (Romans 8:19-27)

As a fellowship of believers, the church is the agent of God. The church is people! The church is not a building, however impressive it may be.

A church building is only a shell. It has no other function but to provide a meetingplace for worship and service. Only the purpose of honoring God makes the structure a sanctum. In it people meet God.

Just as the Church of Christ is not a building, neither is the church the bylaws and doctrines that establish it as an organization.

Bylaws are man-made, and so are doctrines. Bylaws give the church legal status in the world. Through them, the organization and its members have the privilege to enforce rights and obligations in a court of law. Whereas bylaws are a concrete entity in the world, doctrines depend on an obedient response from people in order for them to be meaningful. They exist for the control of spiritual behavior in the membership. Like all other unwritten agreements, they also depend on respect and trust. In this sense alone are doctrines effective in influencing the membership. But sometimes they accomplish even more than written laws. Because doctrines deal in spiritual unknowns, they work on people in the manner of intimidation and fear.

Nor is the church an organization whose prime ambition is to perpetuate itself. Such an entity exerts authoritative pressure over the lives of God's people through fear and threats. Rules and regulations are the product of people. They are contrary to the love of God in Christ Jesus.

Attempts to equate human regulations with God's expectations and Mosaic Law cloud the issue of faithfulness and obedience to God with worldly compliance to conventions and norms of behavior. When Christ repudiated human traditions (Matthew 15:1-9), he condemned spiritual insensitivity. St. Paul expands on this theme by comparing the wisdom of God to human knowledge: "For the word of the cross is folly to those who are perishing, but to us who are being saved it is the power of God. For it is written, 'I will destroy the wisdom of the wise, and the cleverness of the clever I will thwart.' Where is the wise man? Where is the scribe? Where is the debater of this age? Has not God made foolish the wisdom of the world? For since, in the wisdom of God, the world did not know God through wisdom, it pleased God through the folly of what we preach to save those who believe. For Jews demand signs and Greeks seek wisdom, but we preach Christ crucified, a stumbling block to Jews and folly to Gentiles, but to those who are called, both Jews and Greeks, Christ the power of God and the wisdom of God. For the foolishness of God is wiser than men, and the weakness of God is stronger than men." (1 Corinthians 1:18-25)

This analogy coincides with Christ's statement that people can be known through what they do and say: "The good man out of his good treasure brings forth good, and

the evil man out of his evil treasure brings forth evil. I tell
you, on the day of judgment men will render account for
every careless word they utter; for by your words you will
be justified, and by your words you will be condemned."
(Matthew 12:35-36)

The true Church of Christ is an assembly of people in
which faith in Christ is practiced as faithfulness and obedience to God in worship and service. The true church
enlightens people by providing the opportunity for the
Holy Spirit to reveal the truth about God.

Only the truth of the Word of God can set people free.
Jesus Christ made this point perfectly clear when He stated
it as the benefit of discipleship: "If you continue in my
word, you are truly my disciples, and you will know the
truth, and the truth will make you free." (John 8:31-32)

Expanding on Christ's statement, St. Paul wrote to the
Church at Corinth: "Now the Lord is the Spirit, and where
the Spirit of the Lord is, there is freedom." (2 Corinthians
3:17)

Let us reflect on the purpose of our assembly in the
name of Christ. We must examine whether we truly carry
the Christian banner high above all our idiosyncracies and
let the Word of God be our guiding light.

As members of the true church of Christ we must not let
ourselves become entrapped in the muddied waters of
worldly theology.

The Word of God is more important than our earthly
safety or security. The Word of God is absolute in value
over our pride. Followers of Christ must let the light of
Christ shine through them so that ignorance becomes exposed and destroyed.

Ignorance continues to enslave people even today. Its
enchanting stories never allow truth to be known so that
faith can develop. Mysticism is allowed to flourish wherever people fail to reach for the truth of the Word of God.

The "mysterious" has been purposely designed into some church doctrines to make assertions about God. This despite the fact that God has demonstrated divine presence in faithful believers. God is beyond all concepts and images. The God of the Bible is the God of revelation.

Today's mysticism continues to uphold some old precepts. But there is reform to clear up misunderstandings. The veneration of holy places, saints, and relics continues to a lesser degree. The doctrine of the Virgin Mary is being examined to remove a major stumbling block in modern ecumenism.

When the church realizes its existence under grace it then will know peace, because the love of God is at the center of the church. And Jesus Christ is its Lord.

As Christians we are kept safe in the world by the peace of God until Christ takes us unto Himself. St. Paul writes to the Church at Philippi: "And the peace of God, which passes all understanding, will keep your hearts and your minds in Christ Jesus." (Philippians 4:7)

The true church knows that its only mission is to witness to the Lordship of Jesus Christ. Whenever it works this mission under the guiding control of the Holy Spirit, then it shows potential for future and growth. Without the Holy Spirit the church is nothing more than an organization that may call itself improperly by that name.

If the church is to be an agent in the Kingdom of God on earth, then it must carry the message of the Good News of the Gospel of Christ through the revelation of truth. Let there be no doubt that without the Holy Spirit the church is but an organization that provides the opportunity for certain social functions. The church then is an institution of society whose asset on the spiritual balance sheet is a big zero. This organization does not know Christ. Nor does it truly worship God.

The church as the agent of God is a united gathering of

believers. Within this circle of people, faith captures the true vision of God's work to be done. Its unity of spirit sees and recognizes the objective of greater accomplishments on behalf of Christ and the Kingdom of God.

This fellowship is blessed to know God's purpose and subsequently fulfills its assumed responsibilities through its privileged status of restored fellowship. It then exercises its role of leadership. Its teaching is for the sole purpose of giving glory to God.

The leadership role closely resembles the model of the godly life as demonstrated by Jesus Christ. It reflects the new life in the Spirit, which is a life of union with Christ. Its teaching is salvation by grace through faith in Jesus Christ.

Through this teaching the true church declares the Word of God as the power of light over darkness. The Word of God alone can enlighten soul and mind to free it from ignorance. The confession of the true church is God's proclamation that people are set free by God's Spirit from the power of sin and death.

We must recognize the followers of Satan and make known their false teaching. People who say they are disciples of Christ but do not believe in their hearts that "Christ Jesus came into the world to save sinners" (1 Timothy 1:15) are liars and the truth of the Word of God is not in them.

The Church of Christ is like a flock of sheep. Jesus Christ is the shepherd. In this simile rests the fundamental truth of our relationship with God and with one another. The sheep is a symbol of meekness. It lives in demonstration of humility. It has no other desires but to follow the shepherd. When Christ calls believers sheep, we are told what is expected of us. We must follow Christ's leadership in a way that sets the example for others to follow.

Let us consider the authority of institutions, including

the church, in the affairs of family life. There are no justifiable reasons for civil or ecclesiastical organizations to assume influence or control over family life. Worldly measures do not compare to God's expectations. These are not capable of satisfying the spiritual needs of people. Authority in the family has its foundation in love. Ecclesiastical organizations function according to doctrine and policy. And governments exist for the purpose of law and order.

Therefore, organized religion or civil authorities cannot be a substitute to assume the responsibility to help people grow in faith and increase in the knowledge of God. These obligations rest within families.

But authority and responsibility must be defined, understood, and rules for accountability established so that all members in a given society have the same opportunity to determine their destiny. This does not mean that we must sit idly by when innocent people are victimized by their own families. We get involved to help families stay together and aid them to remain viable in the world.

Organized groups cannot dispense love in the same successful way that a healthy family does. Yet organized religion has been exercising spiritual authority over individuals and families through marriage annulments, excommunications, and denials of Holy Communion. Legal intervention for the purpose of law, order, and justice is the duty of society. But when it comes to spiritual control, we must realize that the Holy Spirit alone helps maintain family harmony and coherence.

In the institutional society, love has become formalized in rules and regulations. These are then advanced in systems of law for the purpose of providing order, or in the doctrines of the institutional church to control the faith life.

In either circumstance we will find that faithfulness and obedience to God is being neglected. Prime attention is diverted from the Word of God to a system of law, order, and doctrine. The main objective is to put the organization in the forefront: "This is the position of the church . . . this is its teaching, etc."

Families are the networks of society. But society can neither create nor maintain families. People devoted to God do, for Christ is in the midst of family life.

People who have decided to live according to the ways of the world do not want to acknowledge this important truth. The institutions that society has set up are more meaningful to them than belief and trust in God. Human beings are dependent creatures, and are guided either by the philosophy of the world or by the Word of God. Love for God is perfected when believers obey God's Word.

Organizations in institutional societies are protective of their ways and systems. Contrary to any claims about openmindedness, there is scorn when rules and regulations are challenged. Religious organizations suffer from similar shortcomings. Churches are very protective of doctrines and decrees. When they feel threatened by the truth of the Word of God, they just issue additional decrees in defense of the organization. This we have clearly seen during the events of Luther's Reformation. The Roman Catholic Church excommunicated him because of his differing viewpoints.

Ecclesiastical decrees which do not have as their purpose the needs of the Kingdom of God and God's message of the Gospel that Jesus Christ died for the forgiveness of sins are provocative decrees. Their sole function is to control the membership. For example, God's plan of salvation by grace through faith was masked until recently in the Roman Catholic Church through upholding the principle of "good works."

Institutional society with its laws and doctrines, will

never succeed the family as prescribed by God. The sooner this fact is realized, the quicker the healing process within the family and society as a whole can start. Isaiah described God's desire for humanity's purity: "Come now, let us reason together, says the LORD: though your sins are like scarlet, they shall be as white as snow; though they are red like crimson, they shall become like wool. If you are willing and obedient, you shall eat the good of the land; but if you refuse and rebel, you shall be devoured by the sword; for the mouth of the LORD has spoken." (Isaiah 1:18-20)

We must, therefore, let the Holy Spirit guide the church and the family as God's agents. Those in worldly authority must not supplant the Spirit's control. Ecclesiastical decrees are useless for helping anyone to know God; and human knowledge is inadequate for guiding sinners in the obligation of what God requires of them.

12

God's Truth

Education helps to strengthen faith, but it is faith that secures our unwavering confidence in God. Believers then practice God's will faithfully and obediently.

Knowledge dispels fears. This further strengthens faith.

Christ expects us to search for the truth about God and know its value for the new life in the Spirit. This is a natural request for Christians so that we can share as Christ's disciples the fullness of God's grace through a life that is enveloped in divine wisdom.

The truth about God is the wisdom revealed by the Holy Spirit. We receive this wisdom whenever we become enlightened through knowledge about God.

Our happiness is complete because the Holy Spirit is our guide and companion. Christ tells us that the Holy Spirit "dwells with you, and will be in you." (John 14:17)

There can be no greater satisfaction in life than knowing God's presence. We will experience this assurance whenever we accept the Holy Spirit's guidance to lead us in a life pleasing to God. Our life is complete when we are found acceptable in God's sight.

With this knowledge before us, life on earth can now rest in the peace that Christ has given believers as divine blessing: "Peace I leave with you; my peace I give to you; not as the world gives do I give to you. Let not your hearts be troubled, neither let them be afraid." (John 14:27)

Through our study of the Scriptures, we see the mysticism of blind faith evaporate and sense it being replaced by God's power of truth. We now can give full glory to Christ. Our objectives in life are now similar to what the Holy Spirit does at Christ's bidding: "He will glorify me, for he will take what is mine and declare it to you. All that the Father has is mine; therefore I said that he will take what is mine and declare it to you." (John 16:14-15)

The realization of God's presence is also the moment of deliverance from the power of evil and all its forces of darkness. When we learn to trust God, we will further apppreciate the new confidence we gain from growth in faith.

This process eventually leads to a total dependence on God as the Holy Spirit "will guide you into all the truth; for he will not speak on his own authority, but whatever he hears he will speak, and he will declare to you the things that are to come." (John 16:13) This revelation by the Holy Spirit is God's special class in spiritual education.

Education is God's answer to mysticism and fear. Only when the eyes of the soul are opened, can people give full praise to God. We, then, can indeed echo the words of St. Paul: "O the depth of the riches and wisdom and knowledge of God! How unsearchable are his judgments and how inscrutable his ways! 'For who has known the mind of the Lord, or who has been his counselor? Or who has given a gift to him that he might be repaid?' For from him and through him and to him are all things. To him be glory for ever. Amen." (Romans 11:33-36)

The confidence that we then have in our hearts is worth more than all the power on earth. Earth is but a small part of God's creation. With the Psalmist we will then also repeat the praises of God. Thanksgiving is a daily confession:

"God is our refuge and strength, a very present help in trouble. Therefore we will not fear though the earth should change, though the mountains shake in the heart of the sea; though its waters roar and foam, though the mountains tremble with its tumult." (Psalm 46:1-3)

Through grace and faith, believers will now share divine wisdom. God's invitation to learn universal truth has been made to all people: "Come, behold the works of the LORD, how he has wrought desolations in the earth. He makes wars cease to the end of the earth; he breaks the bow, and shatters the spear, he burns the chariots with fire! 'Be still, and know that I am God. I am exalted among the nations, I am exalted in the earth!' " (Psalm 46:8-10)

We have looked at education as our obligation in our new life in the Spirit. The truth of the Word of God helps us to overcome barriers. It widens horizons for a deeper and more meaningful faith. Ignorance is a tool of Satan, but the Word of God is "the sword of the Spirit." (Ephesians 6:17)

Let us remember, therefore, that "the word of God is living and active, sharper than any two-edged sword, piercing to the division of soul and spirit, of joints and marrow, and discerning the thoughts and intentions of the heart." (Hebrews 4:12)

We have a common saying in the world that education is a life-long process. Indeed, education must never become neglected. A keen mind is a God-given talent to demonstrate God's glory on earth.

With increased knowledge through learning we also gain in wisdom as we come to realize to how little we really know. Only a fool will display his knowledge arrogantly.

When we come to realize our obligation to gain knowledge for the good of ourselves and our fellow men by making the world a better place to live, we then can truly say that our process of education has begun. Our education then is like a part of David's Song of Praise: "I delight to do thy will, O my God; thy law is within my heart." (Psalm 40:8)

13

Work

God has given us talent and strength to work on behalf of the Kingdom of Heaven. We have received these blessings for the sake of God's righteousness. We must use them to bring him honor and glory.

We live and work in faith. Any work that is not motivated in faith to strengthen our relationship with God is wasted effort. Any meaning of our labor can only come from God.

God has placed people on earth for a purpose. Work, therefore, must reflect our status as servants of God. We must live the discipleship that we confess.

Believers are apostles of Christ who are "servants of Christ and stewards of the mysteries of God. Moreover it is required of stewards that they be found trustworthy." (1 Corinthians 4:1-2)

We must give of ourselves to bring glory to God. This truth is emphasized by St. Paul in his teaching: "Do you not know that your body is a temple of the Holy Spirit within you, which you have from God? You are not your own; you were bought with a price. So glorify God in your body." (1 Corinthians 6:19-20)

It is so easy for us to become absorbed in life. Preoccupation with self is then confused with work. Therefore, let us remember that any activity that does not have a set goal is like the flapping of the wings by a bird, who flutters a lot in the air but is flying nowhere.

We are like the bird when we aimlessly drift in life. This must not be. God has redeemed humanity for the purpose of the Gospel and not for self-satisfaction.

Thus, St. Paul writes to the Church at Corinth that he is "under orders" figuratively and actually to preach the Gospel of Christ:

"For Christ did not send me to baptize but to preach the gospel, and not with eloquent wisdom, lest the cross of Christ be emptied of its power." (1 Corinthians 1:17) Because we are also disciples of Christ, as Paul was, we also come under Christ's command to "Go therefore and make disciples of all nations . . . ." (Matthew 28:19)

Christ's charge is specific!

So let us take the directive seriously and prepare ourselves for the work that God has set before us. This is similar to the preparation of an athlete in anticipation of winning the big race. The words of St. Paul are quite descriptive: "Every athlete exercises self-control in all things. They do it to receive a perishable wreath, but we an imperishable. Well, I do not run aimlessly, I do not box as one beating the air; but I pommel my body and subdue it, lest after preaching to others I myself should be disqualified." (1 Corinthians 9:25-27)

Through preparation, we are in a position to bring about rightful glory to God. We can be certain that God will then accept our labors and additionally sanctify us because of them.

Our labors are put in proper perspective by St. Paul. He tells us that "as servants of God we commend ourselves in every way: through great endurance, in afflictions, hardships, calamities, beatings, imprisonments, tumults, labors, watching, hunger; by purity, knowledge, forbearance, kindness, the Holy Spirit, genuine love, truthful speech, and the power of God; with the weapons of righteousness for the right hand and for the left; in honor and dishonor, in ill repute and good repute." (2 Corinthians 6:4-8)

But St. Paul also demonstrates a conflict. As disciples of Christ, and as laborers in God's Kingdom, believers must condition themselves for both appreciation and scorn. Paul gives us a detailed account of the extremes of human behavior: "We are treated as impostors, and yet are true; as unknown, and yet well known. . . ." (2 Corinthians 6:8-9)

But our allegiance to God is stronger than the reaction of people who do not appreciate the Good News of the Gospel of Christ. Through his commitment to Christ, St. Paul feels the assurance of God's Spirit: Although "dying, and behold we live; as punished, and yet not killed; as sorrowful, yet always rejoicing; as poor, yet making many rich; as having nothing, and yet possessing everything." (2 Corinthians 6:9-10)

Let us take the writing of St. Paul as the indication that our work will not always be successful. The reward for our labor is not going to come automatically like the compensation of a wage earner who can count on the weekly paycheck and put the money in the bank. But, on the other hand, discipleship in Christ is not just a work assignment, it is a way of life! More than that even, it is life itself!

Under a work contract, we receive steady compensation in the form of a periodic paycheck. This is not at all the case in discipleship. The mutual concern of God and faithful believers is not recorded on paper with ink. The covenant between God and people is forever sealed with the blood of Christ.

Under the terms of God's grace, witness and preaching is the investment we make as believers on behalf of Christ. So let us not become discouraged when we see no return. People in the evil of their human nature have rejected God since creation. They rejected God with the crucifixion of Christ. And people continue to reject God today whenever they believe that justification before God can be achieved through good works and push aside salvation by grace through faith.

Christ has forewarned us about the conflict. There will be times without progress or tangible rewards. And at the same time Christ admonishes us not to feel discouraged whenever our labors are not appreciated by those we are trying to serve.

The true follower of Christ receives his reward directly from God. People have no influence over the grace of God. The truth of the Word of God is Christ's teaching: "You received without pay, give without pay." (Matthew 10:8)

That God rewards believers according to grace is the message in Christ's explanation of what the Kingdom of heaven is like. In the story about the laborers in the vineyard, Christ distinctly indicates that compensation for our work on behalf of his Kingdom is through the generosity of God (Matthew 20:1-16).

This may be hard to understand. It is contrary to common sense. The greed of human nature forces us to slave and at the same time expects to get handsomely compensated for it.

Let there not be any doubt concerning God's blessing. It can be neither the fruit of any human labor or the result of any of our claims.

In the Kingdom of heaven we receive grace. In it we live by grace. And we do all our work at the bidding of God in Christ. We are acknowledged in the sight of God through grace alone.

Confusion has been perpetuated in groups that have insisted on good works as essential for salvation instead of witnessing to the truth of God's Word that salvation is by grace through faith in Jesus Christ. And this issue has been totally taken out of context by greedy advocates— Christians and nonbelievers alike—who constantly work the rule to get the most out of people. They assert that a wholesome attitude toward one's job includes hard work.

The exploitation of people is an ongoing process. A modern day sweat shop has little or no concern for the well-being of workers. They become satisfied with minimum standards in working conditions and wages. Sometimes the lot of such workers has been improved through unionization.

But today's world also suffers from workaholics. These unfortunate individuals actually believe that the pain of hard labor is pleasing to God. This is not true. When friends, who are concerned about such a person's well-being, point out this fault, the workaholic becomes angry about the interference. People react in a highly defensive manner to our prodding because no one can run away from the guilt feeling that the addiction to work is generating. Hard work is not a substitute for our obligations to God, family, and even ourselves.

Our insistence that hard work is pleasing to God is sin. Our silly reasoning wishes to get God off our backs. The outcome is Christ's judgment because God did not ordain hard work to be the replacement for the purpose of our creation. At the Day of Judgment all people must explain their use of God's gift of time.

Many social ills are caused by the enticement of Satan, through which he appeals to human greed as man's lowest animal instinct. Work, greed, and instinct for survival can be problems of grave concern as we go about to satisfy the needs of family and personal ambition.

14

Government

1. The Role of Government

"And they sent to him some of the Pharisees and some of
the Herodians, to entrap him in his talk. And they came
and said to him, 'Teacher, we know that you are true, and
care for no man; for you do not regard the position of men,
but truly teach the way of God. Is it lawful to pay taxes to
Caesar, or not? Should we pay them, or should we not?'
But knowing their hypocrisy, he said to them, 'Why put me
to the test? Bring me a coin, and let me look at it.' And they
brought one. And he said to them, 'Whose likeness and
inscription is this?' They said to him, 'Caesar's.' Jesus said
to them, 'Render to Caesar the things that are Caesar's, and
to God the things that are God's'." (Mark 12:13-17)

And Jesus plainly told Pilate: "My kingship is not of this
world; if my kingship were of this world, my servants would
fight, that I might not be handed over to the Jews; but my
kingship is not from the world . . . . For this I was born,
and for this I have come into the world, to bear witness to
the truth. Every one who is of the truth hears my voice."
(John 18:36,37)

Government is an institution of the world. It exists by
authority of the people it represents. Its function is to
preside over the affairs of society so that order is main-
tained through a system of law and justice. Government

further administers the responsibility of the people and provides for public welfare for those in need.

The laws that government rules by are commonly derived from experience of problem situations. These are mostly written to correct the shortcomings in social behavior. The intent of these laws is to project a better life for the future.

Laws are designed to give all people in a democratic society equal opportunity in the sharing of rights and obligations. Whereas the world depends on physical strength to make its system work, God's Commandments override human wisdom (Exodus 19-24).

For example, God's rescue of the Israelites from slavery in Egypt has prompted Covenant and Law. Because of people's failure to live by God's standards, God intervened again. And the life, death, and resurrection of Jesus Christ are now part of humanity's history. Through them we also now have the model of the godly life before us. And the teaching about how believers are restored for sharing life with each other in God's presence (Romans 5:1-11) is God's message in the Gospel.

Through this knowledge of divine expectations and similar appreciation of civil laws, people within a given society can then adjust their behavior. An orderly people conforms to accepted norms and standards.

Enlightened government envisions a better way of life through the laws that it dictates. Its laws establish rules for relationships. They appropriate resources wisely. And they look protectively after the people, environment, and material blessings.

On the other hand, a bad government reacts to the matters at hand irrationally. Its laws reflect panic and confusion. In the following chaos, the most severe laws are selected as the instrument to rule people in tyranny. Confusion and chaos are the breeding grounds for conversions from democracy to autocracy.

A beneficient government knows how to maintain order through its laws by enforcing them justly. It recognizes the value of justice as a mechanism for controlling human behavior. Any enlightened society then becomes a dynamic force that establishes its own sphere of influence so that other societies will want to follow its model. When this happens, its status increases and the security of its people is strengthened.

The ideal rule by government has yet to be demonstrated in the world. Daily struggles toward this goal make up the crucial difference between "should" and what is. Even the most advanced democratic state—where citizens enjoy freedom of expression and find appreciation for excellence—looks at utopia as a far-out concept.

Nevertheless, good government should strive to provide order through justice according to laws that are an agglomeration of the best available knowledge. These must be considerate and protective of the future. Good laws should incorporate all experiences of human behavior to prevent undesirable repercussions.

The complement of good laws and good government is necessary for the future and growth of any society. This comes about when laws are evolutionary. Stability and progress provide the foundation for closing the gap between what is ideal and current fact—progress transforms the "should" in government action to the reality of daily life.

Built into the laws, and standing behind the enforcing government, is the authority of the people. Government and law are inseparable. One is the other's disciplined complement. Both should be established for the sole purpose of serving the people. The definite function of gov-

ernment is to maintain order by providing justly for all
people.

2. *Public Trust and Definition of Purpose*

Law, order, and justice are the prime functions of any
government.

A government's strength rests in the pertinence of the
laws to the problems at hand. As the responsible authority
to provide order through justice, government must stay
dynamic by virtue of evolution in its systems of laws.

But as society progresses to new norms of behavior and
updates its laws, government must act to protect the fundamental rights that are basic to ensuring human dignity.
Because these are God-given rights, any government that
recognizes the authority of God as the fundamental responsibility of its people is ruling according to wisdom and will
be blessed with power.

Inasmuch as people have the responsibility to submit
themselves totally to the authority of God, government has
no right to dictate to its people anything that will affect, or
can influence, spiritual performance or eternal destiny.
The Kingdom of God and human organizations in the world
are two separate entities. They are not only separate, but
they are diametrically opposed to each other. The spirit
indeed has superiority over the flesh. And the immortal
prevails over the mortal.

Law, order, and justice, as incorporated in government,
are to the world what the grace of God is to the Kingdom of
heaven. As an institution of the world, government is the
instrument of people. The people are responsible for government. And the government is accountable to the
people, for it has received their authority as a matter of
public trust.

Because government is a dominant force in contemporary life, it will benefit everyone to study its role and our involvement in it. We soon will discover that common to both people and nations is self-preservation. Modern man is not exempt from basic animal instincts. And neither has humanity suffered throughout the ages from a shortage of greed and lust for power.

In writing to the Church at Rome, St. Paul gives a cursory review of a Christian's duties toward state authorities (Romans 13).

Paul speaks about personal behavior in any orderly society. He deliberately avoids fixing a burden of proof—with regard to responsibility and accountability—on those who govern. St. Paul points to the performance of people.

Paul discusses a Christian's involvement in government in terms of the consequences of good and evil behavior. But our compliance to his warning that we must "show respect and honor" toward those who govern suddenly shifts responsibility and accountability from a believer's role to a servant's status.

St. Paul writes: "Therefore he who resists the authorities resists what God has appointed, and those who resist will incur judgment. For rulers are not a terror to good conduct, but to bad. Would you have no fear of him who is in authority? Then do what is good, and you will receive his approval, for he is God's servant for your good. But if you do wrong, be afraid, for he does not bear the sword in vain; he is the servant of God to execute his wrath on the wrongdoer. Therefore, one must be subject, not only to avoid God's wrath but also for the sake of conscience." (Romans 13:2-5)

Honor and respect extended by God's chosen people according to divine decree has suddenly turned into the "double-edged sword" over those in authority. What is freely given must be responsibly administered.

God complied with the wishes of Israel for a king (1

Samuel 8:22). Does this mean that God did not care any more? Far from it. God tolerates coexistence of good and bad people. But at the end of time all people must stand before God in judgment. Christ's parable about the Kingdom of Heaven exemplifies this point (Matthew 13:47-50).

Saul was an expert in the ways of the world. He knew what pleased people. For the sake of popularity, he sacrificed spiritual integrity and the authority of God's prophet (1 Samuel 13:7b-14). Saul's roller coaster performance met God's judgment as he and his sons died on Mount Gilboa (1 Samuel 31:1-6).

By the example of Saul, we are again shown that God's interest is not embodied in the charisma of people, but in faithfulness and obedience to his will and purpose: "Has the LORD as great delight in burnt offerings and sacrifices, as in obeying the voice of the LORD? Behold, to obey is better than sacrifice, and to hearken than the fat of rams. For rebellion is as the sin of divination, and stubbornness is as iniquity and idolatry. Because you have rejected the word of the LORD, he has also rejected you from being king." (1 Samuel 15:22-23)

The strength of any nation is the wisdom of its people. Governments are not made by wishful thinking or meaningless rhetoric. Never-ending promises seldom see the light of day.

People must learn to protect themselves from political theatrics and not become gullible to such trickery. We have been blessed with the truth about God through the Holy Spirit living in us for the purpose of doing the will of God. How, then, can we be faithful and obedient to God when we allow ourselves to be swayed by human nature? We must control human nature and not make it our master. For this very reason we have received newness of life in the Spirit to properly use the power of God.

The power of God is made available to us by the revelation of the Holy Spirit. Christ said that the Holy Spirit "will take what is mine and declare it to you." (John 16:14) The authority that we yield at the ballot box to elect our government is a definite part of this God-given power.

Our responsibility, then, definitely is to God. We are in no way accountable to man for something we have received from God. The right definition of authority in government then is authority by the people. When all realize this obligation, then government works on behalf of the people, doing exactly what they dictate.

3. Our Burden of Responsibility

Whenever people neglect their God-given responsibility, they similarly abdicate their authority to govern themselves. This change can take place through action or inaction at the ballot box, and the function of government can become changed from service to rule.

Our responsibility in the election process is just one part of our overall obligation as children of God. There are many lessons in the Bible to show how Israel's survival depended on loyalty to God, while disloyalty always led to disaster. The stories of Judges show the disaster that came when God's people turned away from Him.

Let us review the instructions to the Israelites concerning the type of life God expected them to lead in the Promised Land: "Take heed to yourself, lest you make a covenant with the inhabitants of the land whither you go, lest it become a snare in the midst of you. You shall tear down their altars, and break their pillars, and cut down their Ashe'rim (for you shall worship no other god, for the LORD, whose name is Jealous, is a jealous God), lest you make a covenant with the inhabitants of the land, and when they play the harlot after their gods and sacrifice to their gods and one invites you, you eat of his sacrifice, and you take of their daughters for your sons, and their daughters play the harlot after their gods and make your sons play the harlot after their gods." (Exodus 34:12-16)

But the people did not take their burden of responsibility seriously, and the beginning of disaster shows Israel's indictment. The angel of the LORD went from Gilgal to Bochim and said to the Israelites: "I brought you up from Egypt, and brought you into the land which I swore to give to your fathers. I said, 'I will never break my covenant with you, and you shall make no covenant with the inhabitants of this land; you shall break down their altars.' But you have not obeyed my command." (Judges 2:1-2)

National disaster came upon the Israelites when they stopped worshiping God after the death of Joshua and began to serve local pagan gods. "So the anger of the LORD was kindled against Israel, and he gave them over to plunderers, who plundered them; and he sold them into the power of their enemies round about, so that they could no longer withstand their enemies." (Judges 2:14)

And the continuous story shows that Israel forgot God again and again. But in the same accounts we also read how the Israelites cried out to God and on every occasion "he sent a man who freed them." The writing in Judges gives valiant accounts about Othniel, Ehud, Deborah and Barak, and some more popular heroes like Gideon and Samson.

But the Book of Judges also contains the dedicated efforts of eleven tribes and their fight against evil. The nation rightfully assumed the sexual abuse and murder of the Levite's wife as a national problem when they set out to rid the land of this evil and purified the faith. Commitment to God overshadowed their sorrow of having totally destroyed the tribe of Benjamin—save for 600 men—and it guided them in making provision so that the Benjaminites would not become extinct (Judges 19-21).

Today's Christians also know of their responsibility to God because of Christ's teaching, but we have an additional obligation to society because our freedom is based on a system of law which all people must uphold and support in order to benefit from this freedom.

The point that must be raised is whether individuals in a free society of God-fearing people have the right to abdicate their responsibility and give away their authority. As God-fearing people, do we have a right to deprive government leadership of best available talent and elect as leaders people who have many shortcomings? Let there not be any doubt, the burden and the responsibility is ours.

We have looked at the method by which government operates as a matter of public trust. Its nature is definitely a reflection of the character of its people. If the government looks sick, then the people surely require healing.

But we are too quick to explain our shortcoming by claiming that we were misled by false promises. Thus, we help set our own trap and then complain when we fall into it. Because we live in the world, we are wise to the world. Surely, we are familiar with the old tricks of stealing from Peter to pay Paul. But this is exactly the essence behind smooth-talking rhetoric that contains promises without any substance. It is our duty, therefore, to clamp down on any irresponsible actions, those in word as well as those in deed. But we don't. We overlook them, simply because by chance we may benefit by them.

Freedom degenerates as people wrongly think that they can afford it because they enjoy prosperity. But as we allow this to happen, government will claim credit for accomplishments, while at the same time flexing its muscle to show the world that it is in full charge. It alone has the authority and the power to rule. And the people will face very convincing arguments that a particular government should continue because it has all the necessary expertise in dealing with the wealth and the power of its people.

It is during these times of false prosperity that the nation will sink to its lowest level because power becomes abused. The consequence is that the poor in the land lose all support. The prosperous do not care, as long as they are taken care of. They do not suffer, although they wish some of the burdens to be lighter. Additionally, there is then no concern for future generations. Selfishness only strives to satisfy immediate demands.

Let us now clear up one of the greatest misconceptions since free society has been ruling itself. This is the notion that government is power and wealth. This is absolutely not true.

Government does not create power and wealth. If anything, it dilutes it.

Power and wealth are the resources of people. But because government is very arrogant, it wants to claim credit during times of prosperity. It readily reacts to praise. And it even more quickly responds when it comes to denying any responsibility for bad times. So we see politicians reacting whenever the floodlights are on problems.

Especially is this the case when these problems were created by the very acts of government and for which those in ruling authority should stand up as being responsible. It is easier to take credit than to accept blame. And the ruling body that once pretended to be so powerful now manufactures whimsical excuses as explanations why certain things happen the way they do.

Government is strong by virtue of the strength of the nation. But the strength of government is not at all a reason for its existence. Power and strength are only useful when wisdom to use them rightfully is present. It is a true saying that wisdom is power and knows how to handle it—but power without wisdom can bring about oppression and tyranny.

The public trust as the authority that people give their elected representatives should be a matter of wisdom and should not be acquired on the basis of cheap rhetoric and empty promises. The authority that rules under the umbrella of wisdom rules also in humility. Wisdom and humility should be partners! Only when they are does representative government provide service that is beneficial to its people.

There is nothing magical about this. This is exactly the objective for electing the government in the first place: To serve its people!

It must not be otherwise. Election to public office is an honor to serve all people justly in the confidence of humility, thus not taking anything for granted in return. Election to public office is an honor that costs dearly. It carries the burden to serve wisely, for the decisions of government have far-reaching consequences into the future.

The government must protect all its people. Through its system of laws it provides order as it justly administers the behavior of people. But a government's responsibility does not extend outside its own society.

Neither does government have any authority to regulate, by law or suggestion, the important relationship of God and man. Government rules in the world. But God, as the Creator of heaven and earth, is ruler of all. All matters concerning the spirit come under the authority given to

Christ. Our resurrected Lord clearly assumed all responsibility on behalf of believers: "All authority in heaven and on earth has been given to me" (Matthew 28:18) was Christ's confirmation to instill hope in apostles and disciples. And Christ substantiated the words of hope with the promise to guide our lives: "I am with you always, to the close of the age." (Matthew 28:20)

15

Justice

"But he who looks into the perfect law, the law of liberty, and perseveres, being no hearer that forgets but a doer that acts, he shall be blessed in his doing." (James 1:25)

Speaking on the subject of the final judgment, Jesus says: "When the Son of man comes in his glory, and all the angels with him, then he will sit on his glorious throne. Before him will be gathered all the nations, and he will separate them one from another as a shepherd separates the sheep from the goats, and he will place the sheep at his right hand, but the goats at the left. Then the King will say to those at his right hand, 'Come, O blessed of my Father, inherit the kingdom prepared for you from the foundation of the world; for I was hungry and you gave me food, I was thirsty and you gave me drink, I was a stranger and you welcomed me, I was naked and you clothed me, I was sick and you visited me, I was in prison and you came to me.' Then the righteous will answer him, 'Lord, when did we see thee hungry and feed thee, or thirsty and give thee drink? And when did we see thee a stranger and welcome thee, or naked and clothe thee? And when did we see thee sick or in prison and visit thee? And the King will answer them, 'Truly, I say to you, as you did it to one of the least of these my brethren, you did it to me.' (Matthew 25:31-40)

"Then he will say to those at his left hand, 'Depart from me, you cursed, into the eternal fire prepared for the devil and his angels; for I was hungry and you gave me no food, I was thirsty and you gave me no drink, I was a stranger and you did not welcome me, naked and you did not clothe me, sick and in prison and you did not visit me.' Then they also will answer, 'Lord, when did we see thee hungry or thirsty or a stranger or naked or sick or in prison, and did not minister to thee?' Then he will answer them, 'Truly, I say to you, as you did it not to one of the least of these, you did it not to me.' And they will go away into eternal punishment, but the righteous into eternal life." (Matthew 25:41-46)

Through the principles of justice, believers have a perfect opportunity to model their lives on the righteousness of God. Jesus directs his followers that they must do for others what Christ already has done for them, especially now since Christians are also disciples.

We are told that our new existence is a life of freedom in the Spirit. And we are admonished to carry on the work of Christ in faithful and obedient service to God and people. As the truth of the Word of God has brought us peace and spiritual freedom, in like manner must we help others who face oppression and set them free from sin and death.

The part of God's justice that we are charged to help administer is to carry the Cross in Christ's war of light and darkness. With the Cross of Christ, we symbolically represent the truth of the Word of God.

As children of God we must pattern our attitudes after Christ's example of the godly life. In addition, Christ has given us a description of practical piety in the Sermon on the Mount, where Christ introduced the new age and also placed the demand on believers to strive toward the higher righteousness (Matthew 5:1-7:27).

As disciples of Christ we cannot walk away from situations where the truth of the Word of God is not fully known or has been manipulated for evil purposes. This is the burden of responsibility that we carry as Christians. And we are held accountable for our performance.

Our spiritual appreciation of justice sets the tone for making sure that equality before the law is practiced in the world. Justice is instrumental in preserving and maintaining order.

As united people living under the law of the land, we must stand up for the law and defend it against misuse and misrepresentation. We have a duty to help our fellow citizens obtain their rights before the law. Our failure to do so will make us guilty of holding the very same law in utter contempt.

Through education and experience, we have become exposed to the rule of justice. Its principles relate to written laws as well as any accepted norms and standards of society. But since behavioral patterns are not always obvious to all, their value must be established again and again whenever deviations occur.

Since society evolves, any of its norms and standards are by necessity subject to constant revisions. The burden is placed on citizens to employ the principle of justice with the right proportion of wisdom to determine that no fundamental rights are uprooted. This is especially true for people living in a constitutional society. Basic rights are the foundation of freedom.

Any court of law has no choice but to pronounce judgment whenever someone's rights have been attacked. Its judgment must be an impartial evaluation of facts. Justice is served as truth then becomes subject to human wisdom. So we speak often about wise judgments. These decrees have truth and wisdom proportionally meshed to uphold human dignity and value.

Once judgment is pronounced, then justice can be tempered with mercy. But let us realize that mercy goes with justice, not judgment.

Mercy or compassion is a gift of reconciliation offered by the victim, or it may be part of a recommendation by the prosecuting state attorney to the court in offenses against society. This gift is similar to the grace of God by which all sinners are reconciled and restored to fellowship through the forgiveness of sins in Jesus Christ.

Let us recall, though, that "all have sinned and fall short of the glory of God." (Romans 3:23)

If no judgment were pronounced, how would the offender know that he must amend his ways? Any irresponsible failure to prosecute is not only destructive to those who have rejected the law, but is also an offense to society and a direct attack on the public trust.

The value of judgment and justice is brought to light for believers in the spiritual teaching found in the writing of Hebrews: "And have you forgotten the exhortation which addresses you as sons?—'My son, do not regard lightly the discipline of the Lord, nor lose courage when you are punished by him. For the Lord disciplines him whom he loves, and chastises every son whom he receives.' " (Hebrews 12:5-6)

Let us briefly review justice in light of St. Paul's concept of the whole armor of God, about which he writes to the Church at Ephesus. Justice can be compared to "the sword of the Spirit, which is the word of God." (Ephesians 6:17)

And the writer of Hebrews expands on this theme by telling its readers that "the word of God is living and active, sharper than any two-edged sword, piercing to the division of soul and spirit, of joints and marrow, and discerning the thoughts and intentions of the heart." (Hebrews 4:12)

The double-edged sword of justice that we hold in our hands is our responsibility to help procure judgment. And our duty as disciples of Christ demands at the same time that we temper the sentence of judgment with mercy.

Within this understanding, justice is being made a definite part of obedience to God. Full reliance on God alone will make it possible for the Holy Spirit living in us to wield the proper edge of the "double-edged sword."

16

Tension Resulting from
Human Interaction

1. Behavioral Patterns

St. Paul writes to Timothy: "If any one teaches otherwise and does not agree with the sound words of our Lord Jesus Christ and the teaching which accords with godliness, he is puffed up with conceit, he knows nothing; he has a morbid craving for controversy and for disputes about words, which produce envy, dissension, slander, base suspicions, and wrangling among men who are depraved in mind and bereft of the truth, imagining that godliness is a means of gain." (1 Timothy 6:3-5)

St. Paul concludes his message on false teaching and true riches with the categorical pronouncement that the "love of money is the root of all evils." (1 Timothy 6:10a)

This statement serves to condemn all selfish accumulations of wealth. It applies to all people in the world who replace a true relationship with God for material gains. The byproduct of greed is an arrogant dependence on one's abilities to sustain the good life.

The curse that such people live under establishes their final destiny as ultimate death. The riches they have trusted in cannot save them. These "poor" fools really have wasted the opportunity all their lives to be faithful and obedient to God in worship and in service.

Jesus has already stated that true riches cannot be accumulated by people and then transferred to heaven. True wealth is the glory of God reserved for believers at the end of their labor. They were, indeed, concerned above everything else with "his kingdom and his righteousness." (Matthew 6:33)

Christ's parable of the rich fool is putting relationships in proper perspective. The truth of the Word of God condemns all dependence on riches.

Materialistic greed accounts for some present-day difficulties. But the universal problem is not always excess wealth or the sin through which people make riches their sole objective in life. The modern problem is one of economy. There are not always sufficient resources to meet life's needs.

Whatever someone else has in excess is immaterial, unless we desire to complicate our misery further by mixing desperation with envy. Envy is a tool of Satan. Its primary function is to destroy a person's true identity with God through greed. Desperate people then unjustly try to bring someone else's property into their possession.

Economic security is not at all a simple matter of the "haves" and the "have-nots." Economic security is the ability to accept our true status as children of God and then labor in faith because we have divine assurance that God will take care of us.

To receive this support, believers must humble themselves before God and ask for help. The humility of the soul is the most effective prayer. When we approach God in this manner, then we are in harmony with the purpose of our creation and, indeed, have the right attitude as disciples of Christ. God's wealth is available to believers. Jesus is generous: "Whatever you ask in my name, I will do it." (John 14:13)

But this promise by Christ to the disciples is not given to satisfy human greed or lust for riches. We will receive spiritual satisfaction, and all the necessary blessings to successfully live in the world, so "that the Father may be glorified in the Son." (John 14:13)

As children of God, and disciples of Christ, we are blessed with the opportunity to tap the reservoir of God's wealth. It is ours just for the asking. God will supply us in abundance for every occasion where we intend to glorify God through Christ.

When Jesus declared believers free in the Spirit through discipleship, Christ also provided a detailed procedure through which all people can achieve this privileged status: "If you continue in my word, you are truly my disciples, and you will know the truth, and the truth will make you free." (John 8:31-32)

How, then, does the Word of God become reality to believers? By the power of God's Holy Spirit in us! But this is only possible when Jesus Christ is the Lord of our life. This will only happen when a repentant heart seeks the forgiveness of sins and accepts salvation in faith as a gift from God.

Lack of faith in Christ is the crux of all of our problems.

Ignorance is a very efficient tool of Satan through which he makes the rich poor and drives the poor to utter despair. Satan works the tool of ignorance constantly among people to keep priorities scrambled.

Ignorance covers its own ground. Its true identity is always hidden, and a state of confusion continues. This is exactly what the sly serpent wants it to be.

Is it any wonder, then, that people cannot envision goals? They will never fully realize the purpose for life as long as their prime concern is to get past the immediate.

In the midst of this dilemma, Jesus calls us: "Come to

me, all who labor and are heavy laden, and I will give you rest. Take my yoke upon you, and learn from me; for I am gentle and lowly in heart, and you will find rest for your souls." (Matthew 11:28-29)

The yoke of Christ then put upon us is the truth of the Word of God. The yoke figuratively reminds us of our obligation of faithfulness and obedience. We must submit to the Lordship of Christ if our return to fellowship with God is to be the reality of eternal life.

Thus, we have identified the true problem as ignorance. Satan and his tool of ignorance keeps people confused by hiding the truth of the Word of God from them.

We are guilty of collusion with the enemy whenever we preach and teach Christ as a concept instead of the life-giving Spirit of God. As we do this, we water down the Church of the Pentecost celebration with so much spirituality that the Holy Spirit of God is not clearly visible as the power that alone will make us proclaim God's message with boldness.

2. Economic Ills

Not being able to do certain things can force the evil in human nature into the forefront. We are more prone to release our animal instinct than we are willing to adapt to circumstances of hardship. The fact of life is that during economic hardships people must struggle to survive.

Priorities and programs must be rearranged. The daily agenda becomes crowded with value judgments. Decisions will have to be made to establish new priorities and work out affordable solutions.

In addition to helping those in need, let us also examine what must be done to right any wrong done to innocent people. We have failed in our obligation to God when we bypass any injustice to others. Our silence indirectly approves their suffering.

Whenever economic hardship is a national problem, we are involved, even though we may not feel the pain. Our failure to speak up and defend what is right adds to the tensions of others.

Specifically this is the case when economic hardship is caused by government overspending. We are guilty when we allow our government to spend beyond its ability to pay for any programs that may benefit us now but have dire consequences on the livelihood of future generations. We rob our children of their potential in the future by tapping this potential to pay our commitments.

This willful manipulation of the public trust is an abdication of our God-given authority, for which we were created to do God's work faithfully and obediently. Let us recall that God established our relationship on an individual basis. Therefore, how dare we drag future generations, not at all connected with our difficulties, into our specific predicament and thereby dilute God's expectation of us? We alone are responsible for all our actions.

In this great social conflict, we have additional tensions arising from an unwarranted desire to compare ourselves to others. We consume ourselves for the sake of lifting us up above everybody else. In these unfortunate situations, material wealth is taken as the only true measure of success in life. We have easily wiped from memory the fact that real success can only be realized by being faithful and obedient to God.

It is frightening that there are even some world religions that condone this striving for accomplishments, as these "religious" organizations tend to gain also a portion of the accumulated wealth.

For example, worldly religions up to modern times have

fostered economic successes because they also gained when tithing was in effect. Although the custom of tithing today is based on free-will offering, the concept was obligatory by ecclesiastical law in the Western Church from the 6th century until it was eventually abolished throughout Europe during the 19th century.

But the church has also used other tactics to persuade the membership to give for maintaining its organization and also expensive building programs. Some of the church buildings are with us still. Their presences indict the church's call to sacrificial giving, as all of them are out of step with the economic realities of people during the time of construction. Yet, in its line of preaching, the church has always emphasized—as it does today—that "it is better to give than to receive." Organized religion has taken pleas for fiscal support outside the context of the will and purpose of God for taking care of the less fortunate in the land.

For example, a gruesome money-raising campaign some 500 years ago precipitated demands for church reforms. Martin Luther protested spiritual abuses for financial gain in the sale of indulgences. And the failure to correct this wrong again fractured the already split body of Christ.

And in today's world we find many versions of religious cults who are not at all reluctant to demand of their membership. They teach about God by means of convincing arguments that require backing by the checkbook instead of the Bible. Matters really get out of hand when sinners are given false indication of hope through meaningless absolutions. These are implied whenever contributions are praised as a valuable sacrifice.

We must seek divine intervention to give relief for the faithful and the many unfortunate sufferers among us. "God will provide" is the divine promise recorded by the prophets and the assurance given to us by Christ.

We recognize in our prayers those who are innocent victims of reckless decisions. And we ask for God to supply the wisdom to control our lives through the power of the Holy Spirit.

Excess wealth is not the only evil facing people. But responsible management of what God has given us is an opportunity for all believers to show the world their discipleship in Christ so that "they may see your good works and give glory to your Father who is in heaven." (Matthew 5:16)

3. Confronting Evil

We must recognize that we live in this world by the grace of God despite the presence of evil. We are God's instruments to help overcome evil with good. We are reminded of this charge in Christ's prayer, in which he specifically petitioned God the Father on our behalf to "keep them from the evil one." (John 17:15)

Additionally, in the Lord's Prayer, Christ taught us the petition "but keep us save from the evil one." A believer's existence, therefore, is a constant prayer for strength and safety.

The "evil one" is the manifestation of greed and envy in people. Other nations around us envy the strength made up of our resources of materials and people. Our adversaries are devilish antagonists who either want our resources outright or destroy them if they can't get them. In their drive for ultimate control they then destroy happiness and peace.

Any outward aggression is a sign of internal tension that the aggressor cannot cope with. Therefore, any nation trying to subdue its neighbor is directing attention away from its own unresolved problems.

But the conflict that we experience in the world is only a small portion of the overall cosmic engagement of the powers of light and darkness, righteousness and sin, life and death. We will continue feeling the impact of these conflicts in the world until Christ comes and takes us unto Himself.

In the meantime, God's Holy Spirit helps believers to build their trust in God as our confidence in God's protection is reinforced through our study of the Scriptures. In them we find many examples of help that God had provided for the faithful, as for instance, to David.

Our spiritual horizons are widened when we read David's expressions of steadfastness, specifically his public confessions, which are an open record in the Bible. David declared: "For God alone my soul waits in silence, for my hope is from him. He only is my rock and my salvation, my fortress; I shall not be shaken. On God rests my deliverance and my honor; my mighty rock, my refuge is God. Trust in him at all times, O people; pour out your heart before him; God is a refuge for us." (Psalms 62:5-8)

And through the words of the ninety-first Psalm we are led to see the reward of our trust because the Lord indeed supports us: "A thousand may fall at your side, ten thousand at your right hand; but it will not come near you. You will only look with your eyes and see the recompense of the wicked." (Psalms 91:7-8)

Our success in life on earth is a function of the degree of confidence that we have in God to take care of any needs against all onslaught of evil.

As Christians, we know for a fact that the world and all the people in it are God's creation. We further believe that no society or nation has any right to specific claims within God's creation. We all have the opportunity to repent and ask for the forgiveness of sins. Together, then, the people of all nations can claim salvation as a gift because grace is founded on the righteousness of God. The Cross of Christ represents the common base for all of God's people. Divine power unites all Christian believers who assemble beneath the Cross of Christ to hear the Gospel.

But where the Gospel is not preached and Christ's model of the godly life is not the example, tensions will develop that eventually will spill over into other lands. Evil does not recognize boundaries. It just grows naturally, because human nature feeds its greedy demands.

Mankind has advanced in degeneration since the disobedience of Adam. We have found the perfect complement to hypocrisy and false teaching in the greater evil of massive self-destruction. We inflict hardships and pain on ourselves and others through arrogant pride. Instead of exposing our shortcomings, we bury them with destructive force.

This is precisely what war is all about.

War is destructive—more so to our soul than to the physical being. The sacrifice of those innocents killed is then hailed and honored. The pain of this loss is compensated by money as society fulfills its obligation to the survivors.

We honor the brave. We recognize the maimed and temporarily show sorrow for those that continue to suffer by telling them that they saved the country. History then records that the war economy strengthened the nation.

We snarl at those who question the motives of war: "It is not good to have too much negativism," and brand any inquiry as not constructive to patriotism.

Because petitions for victory and peace were never made part of a living relationship with God, people feel no further need to emphasize faithfulness and obedience when war ends, despite the knowledge that the truth of the Word of God demands constant faithfulness, reliance, and dependence on God.

In the purity of our faith we must not forget to constantly petition God to enlighten us with knowledge of divine will and purpose: "Make me to know thy ways, O LORD; teach me thy paths. Lead me in thy truth, and teach me, for thou art the God of my salvation; for thee I wait all the day long." (Psalms 25:4-5)

And as disciples of Christ we know how to praise God in thanksgiving: "The LORD is my light and my salvation; whom shall I fear? The LORD is the stronghold of my life; of whom shall I be afraid?" (Psalms 27:1)

17

The True Value of Earthly Life

The true value of the earthly life is a summary of the activities we perform in honor and praise of God our Creator. We have achieved our mission in life when we know, believe, act, and live according to whose we truly are.

When we realize that we are children of God and, as disciples of Christ, God's chosen people, then we know that we have a relationship of value. In the restored fellowship with God, promises are trusted and commitments are an established routine.

People can slave until their dying day and not know what they have really stood for. We see many examples of utterly despairing life in the world. Masses of people are spiritually confused. They find relief from despair in the small talk of daily life. They lack security and because of it sway with the tides of public opinions.

But discipleship in Christ has provided the model of the godly life. Christians know the way of truth. The steadfastness of true life has been demonstrated by Christ. Our security is the blessing of life in union with Christ. We are free from the curse of trusting in the ways of the world and its schemes for riches and good works. We do not solicit the admiration of people. And we do not go all out to be popular.

Jesus said: "Not every one who says to me, 'Lord, Lord,'

shall enter the kingdom of heaven, but he who does the will of my Father who is in heaven. On that day many will say to me, 'Lord, Lord, did we not prophesy in your name, and cast out demons in your name, and do many mighty works in your name?' And then will I declare to them, 'I never knew you; depart from me, you evildoers.' " (Matthew 7:21-23)

Self-justification will not hold ground. People are put right with God by the free gift of God's grace. True justification is through the righteousness of God.

"True value" is a contradictory expression that is totally useless. This and similar phrases may be a proper choice in advertising, but every place else it is empty talk, unless we qualify its meaning.

"True" implies authenticity. It is something that is conforming to an established standard. Its nature is absolute inasmuch as the standard is authoritative. "Value," on the other hand, is relative. Value can be many things to different people. When something is of value, it then has some worth to the beholder, not necessarily to all. Value is relative to time, place and one's outlook on life.

The true value of the earthly life is our relationship with God here and now. This is as important to us as life itself. It is our pass to eternal life.

Let us recall that the story of mankind is a drama of many tragedies. Its authenticity is attested by many saved or wrecked lives.

We are not the authors of life, but we are the authors of all our shortcomings. Through the frailty of human nature, people continually fail to measure up to the expectation of God. When we study the Scriptures, we can see all the gruesome results of sin and rebellion.

But as we continue, we will find that our life story can have a happy ending because salvation in Jesus Christ is universal. Its truth is eternal.

Let us focus on the act of salvation. About 2000 years ago Christ gave His life to fulfill a promise by God that humanity should again have the opportunity of eternal fellowship in God's presence.

"Stop right there!" you may shout. "What gives you the right to call me a sinner? How nervy can you be? I am an upright citizen, a leader in the community. I do always what is right. I work hard earning a living for my family. I struggle not to rub anyone the wrong way. I try to make friends and keep peace. Even once in a while my family drags me to church, although I must admit that somehow I feel very uneasy when I am there! What more do you want? What else must I give?"

But God wants you! Not your things. Not your good works and accomplishments. God wants you as a person. God provides the return of your spirit! That is why God came down to earth in the person of Jesus Christ to take you back to Himself!

Jesus came for the benefit of people. Christ taught the truth of the Word of God so that everyone who believes in him can be freed from all the hang-ups of the world. These have people so overwhelmed with meaningless concerns that visions into eternity are threatened.

Therefore, Christ says, "If you continue in my word, you are truly my disciples, and you will know the truth, and the truth will make you free." (John 8:31-32)

Jesus did not leave us alone in the world. He asked God to give us a helper and guide. We have God's Holy Spirit among us and in each of us: "And I will pray the Father, and he will give you another Counselor, to be with you for ever, even the Spirit of truth, whom the world cannot receive, because it neither sees him nor knows him; you know him, for he dwells with you, and will be in you." (John 14:16-17)

Only in this has our earthly life true value!

18

War and Peace

1. The Crucial Issue

War is utter futility.

This statement is a summary of experience by innocent victims of war—soldiers and civilians alike. The world is not big enough to contain the necessary comfort in support of people for the upset caused by suffering and death.

Irony crowns all assumptions that there is glory in war. After any conflict, people of ordinary walks of life on either side pick up the broken pieces and work together to heal the wounds of battles. The humble and meek mend what was torn apart by the proud and the strong.

Some people say that wars are just. The attempt to classify wars as just or unjust goes back to ancient times. Issues then were looked at from a theological point of view. In Old Testament times, for example, we read about David's early exposure to battles (1 Samuel 17:17-19). The young lad's job was to bring food to his brothers, who were fighting the Philistines.

The Bible indicts human involvement in war as our inability to get along with one another. For the purpose of clarification, Christ repeated the Laws of Holiness and Justice when giving us the second most important commandment to love our neighbor as we love ourselves: "You shall not hate your brother in your heart, but you shall reason with your neighbor, lest you bear sin because of him. You shall not take vengeance or bear any grudge against the sons of your own people, but you shall love your neighbor as yourself: I am the LORD." (Leviticus 19:17-18)

In war, people glorify destruction and killing for the sake of it. Futility abounds when greed and lust for power motivates the ambition of individuals and nations. Jeremiah's prophecy concerning Moab is God's universal warning to all proud, arrogant, and conceited people: "I know his insolence, says the LORD; his boasts are false, his deeds are false." (Jeremiah 48:30)

Over the past 3000 years, history has witnessed the rise and fall of Assyria, Babylonia, the Persian Empire, Alexander's conquests and the spreading of Greek influence, and the Roman Empire.

From 500 A.D. to 1500 A.D. the world experienced the meddling in political affairs by the popes in Rome. No nation in the Western World exercised authority without ecclesiastical consent.

Modern history contains its share of conflicts and ruthless settlements of people by princes and kings. More recently, World War I—"the war to end all wars"— precipitated World War II and brought on many horrors and merciless suffering. Today's jungle warfare in Africa adds to this sad and futile record. Legions of innocent people have suffered and died because of the attempt by a few individuals to satisfy their greed and lust for power.

Battles may be won, but only Satan benefits from any victories when people attempt to destroy each other. No one will ever realize full satisfaction out of winning a conflict or war, because the greed of human nature is like a bottomless pit.

Yet, we try to fill it! We justify our attempts to satisfy this pit through a neatly compiled summary of reasons. However logical these may sound to us is of no consequence.

Any reasoning to justify war will never prove true on the Day of Judgment. Only when we are called to defend the glory of God is our involvement in war really justified.

When that conflict ends, then Christ will victoriously raise the banner of salvation high on the Cross. And all creation will see that the Day of Judgment has been set for the world (John 16:25-33). This alone can be rightfully called the war to end all wars.

When that time comes, believers will know eternal peace. The hatchet of hate, as an instrument of greed, will be delegated to the eternal fire of hell. And hate will have no more substance left to feed its destructive appetite.

People will give glory to God in constant praise and adoration. Fiery discord will not be kindled anymore. Peace will be realized through complete harmony of our being with God (Isaiah 2:4).

The heart of man will become like a fountain of love from which will flow forth the life-giving water of regeneration. No longer will the heart of man be the breeding ground for future evil (Isaiah 12:1-6).

We are in the world (John 17:15). But we have overcome the world by victoriously rising above it through our life of union with Christ (John 17:21).

Our strength, as well as our true source of peace, is God. God manifested this strength in the person of Jesus Christ. Christ came declaring *war on the evil in our hearts:* "Do not think that I have come to bring peace on earth; I have not come to bring peace, but a sword." (Matthew 10:34)

When all was said and done, Christ left *us* in peace: "Peace I leave with you; my peace I give to you; not as the world gives do I give to you. Let not your hearts be troubled, neither let them be afraid." (John 14:27)

Christ talks about a type of peace that heretofore has not been given. Christ's peace (John 14:27) is the divine gift

that is prompted by our proclamation of Christ as LORD
and made perfect in God's blessing of restored fellowship.
At that moment of spiritual salvation, sin and evil have no
more power over believers.

2.   The Conflict in Man as the Source of War

In total disobedience, Adam rejected the will and purpose of God the Creator. With the disobedience of the man
Adam, humanity was condemned to share the punishment
of missing God's objective in life. Adam and all of humanity
after him was banished from the presence of God. Human
life was limited by God's sentence of judgment.

And ever since then, the downslide of humanity has
continued. Cain permanently punctured the protective
umbrella of the peace of God with the murder of his
brother Abel.

Peace had been ordained by God as a blessing in a life of
devotion to worship and service. But now it was lost.

War and killing is not an evolutionary development. It
was in the first generation of humanity that Cain killed
Abel. This act of selfishness and human greed devoured the
innocent blood of Abel, who knew how to be faithful to God
and live up to God's expectations.

The blood of Christ is given to believers as the seal of a
new covenant with God. In this divine sacrifice, the blood
of Christ fulfills God's promise of life. The grace of God
assures our restored fellowship. Salvation in Christ frees
believers from all past sins. The Good News of the Gospel
is God's message of hope: "You have come to Mount Zion
and to the city of the living God, the heavenly Jerusalem,
and to innumerable angels in festal gathering, and to the
assembly of the first-born who are enrolled in heaven, and
to a judge who is God of all, and to the spirits of just men

made perfect, and to Jesus, the mediator of a new covenant, and to the sprinkled blood that speaks more graciously than the blood of Abel." (Hebrews 12:22-24)

Christ, as the Redeemer of people everywhere, is God's answer to making us perfect again. This provision comes to us through divine grace and is given as an opportunity. But it demands our decision and our faith.

God does not force Himself on people. God looks for a response and commitment of faithfulness and obedience. Yet humanity roams the earth according to its own desires. People forcefully exert their influence over God's creation.

We must be aware of circumstances that will demand that we do the work of God in stopping evil. This point is demonstrated in God's charge to King Saul. When the prophet Samuel anointed Saul, he specifically instructed him to protect God's people "from the hand of their enemies." (1 Samuel 10:1)

But we must realize that any involvement in the fight against Satan and all the forces of darkness is not our battle but the Lord's. We are only instruments to do God's will. Faithfulness to God will bring about God's purpose according to divine plan.

Such obedience, for example, Saul had failed to acknowledge. Consequently, the traps of Satan proved his downfall. And God executed the sentence of divine judgment on Saul at Mount Gilboa (1 Samuel 31:8).

Despite knowledge that God demands obedience, people today continue to act like Saul in their deliberations about future events. Saul reacted to threats instead of acting on the instructions of God.

The prophet Samuel had specifically told Saul to wait for him at Gilgal (1 Samuel 10:8). Samuel was concerned that proper sacrifices be offered to God to show the people that God was leading them into battle.

But Saul was spiritually blinded through his disobedience. He failed to recognize the importance of putting God
first. Self-esteem and popularity were of greater value to
Saul than the will of God. Satan's diversion of unrest among
the people was not a sufficient reason for Saul to abandon
trust in God.

Satan's trap closed permanently on Saul as God pronounced judgment. Through Samuel God wielded the
"double-edged sword": "You have done foolishly; you have
not kept the commandment of the LORD your God, which
he commanded you; for now the LORD would have established your kingdom over Israel for ever. But now your
kingdom shall not continue; the LORD has sought out a
man after his own heart; and the LORD has appointed him
to be prince over his people, because you have not kept
what the LORD commanded you." (1 Samuel 13:13-14)

The choice at the crossroads of life to either go their own
way or consult God in prayer is given entirely to people.
Human beings can either act on the Word of God or react
to the circumstances around them. Like Saul had done at
Gilgal and repeatedly thereafter: "There's no time to consult the LORD!" This expression was like second nature to
Saul.

The command to Saul, "Now go and smite Am'alek, and
utterly destroy all that they have; do not spare them, but
kill both man and woman, infant and suckling, ox and
sheep, camel and ass," (1 Samuel 15:3) was God's renewed
test of obedience.

We again see that Saul succeeded in battle. But Saul
miserably failed in faithfulness to God: "But Saul and the
people spared Agag, and the best of the sheep and of the
oxen and of the fatlings, and the lambs, and all that was
good, and would not utterly destroy them; all that was
despised and worthless they utterly destroyed." (1 Samuel
15:9)

Any rejection of the will of God will bring ultimate judgment. St. Paul tells the Church at Rome that God will eventually give up on us: "And since they did not see fit to acknowledge God, God gave them up to a base mind and to improper conduct." (Romans 1:28)

Finally, God sealed Saul's judgment. The prophet Samuel pronounced the truth of the Word of God: "Has the LORD as great delight in burnt offerings and sacrifices, as in obeying the voice of the LORD? Behold, to obey is better than sacrifice, and to hearken than the fat of rams. For rebellion is as the sin of divination, and stubbornness is as iniquity and idolatry. Because you have rejected the word of the LORD, he has also rejected you from being king." (1 Samuel 15:22-23)

Ever since the day of God's judgment, Saul lived in obsession to kill God's newly anointed shepherd-king David. Arrogant pride and compromise, for the sake of popularity, had destroyed Saul's faithfulness and obedience to God. He was useless for doing God's work.

As it has happened with Saul, we also can make our life unbearable with opposing views about the glory of the Kingdom of God instead of trying to live up to God's expectations. All attempts to outsmart God are futile. Nor can we be all things to all people. Saul tried, and he failed.

Human life is created for the single purpose of being faithful to God. Christ has confirmed this point by living, suffering, and dying in obedience to the Father. In the parable about the shrewd manager, Christ further stresses singlemindedness of purpose: "No servant can serve two masters; for either he will hate the one and love the other, or he will be devoted to the one and despise the other. You cannot serve God and mammon." (Luke 16:13)

Compromise played a role leading up to World War II. The British Prime Minister accommodated the idiosyncracies of a madman as the rest of the world stood idly by.

Accommodation is like a cancer that grows at the expense of truth and principle.

When politics then explode, war is inevitable because emotions are out of control. Participants and onlookers alike then defend their decisions to go into battle because honor and morality demand that all good people fight a just war.

King David, as successor to the unfaithful and disobedient Saul, fought many conflicts. But he was battling the forces of evil around him in the name of God.

His faithfulness and obedience to God led to victories. They proved that David was involved in God's cause. David knew many sorrows. But he also acknowledged God in thanksgiving. The Psalms, as the hymnbook of the Bible, is the record of David's songs of praise.

The shepherd-king knew war. But he also experienced God's blessing of peace on every occasion when he let his life and spirit become engulfed by the love of God.

Whenever Christians are the instruments of God against evil, they can be assured of receiving God's subsequent blessing of peace.

Although David was influenced by human nature and its animal instinct, he never fought battles to subdue other people to get their blessings.

Before any encounter in battle, David always acknowledged his dependence and trust in God. In his determination to do the will of God, David searched actively for God's purpose in his life.

Throughout David's early reign, conflict was God's tool to strengthen his faithfulness and obedience. But it took the story of the lamb to return David to his proper place of relationship with God after his adultery with Bathsheba and the subsequent premeditated murder of Uriah.

David's contrite heart in the prose of the 51st Psalm

satisfied the requirement of repentance as God declared through His prophet: "The LORD also has put away your sin; you shall not die." (2 Samuel 12:13)

Thus, we can readily see that the conflict within man is the source of many troubles, with one another and with other nations. Wars do not just happen. They are created by the devilish schemes of the human mind. Human nature longs for getting by force what God otherwise has chosen to withhold.

3. Theology of the Sword

Whenever there is coercion in the teaching of the Word of God, the Gospel of Christ is misused. Its meaning is changed to a satanic instrument of fear. Such practices must be condemned vehemently.

To invoke divine authority is a natural desire of many people. James and John were drawn into this trap when the Samaritan village refused to receive Jesus. They felt tempted to destroy the inhabitants by calling "fire down from heaven." Christ's rescue is implied in the statement that Jesus "turned and rebuked them." (Luke 9:51-56)

Some modern day preaching delivers an ideology of hell, fire, and brimstone. "Doomsday artists" falsely project their own environment of darkness and misery as theology and as the truth about God. They roam the earth on the strength of personal ambition and charisma in hopes of finding a following who, like them, subscribe to the theme "let's return to the basics" with regard to everyday life. The "new" spirituality they are promoting is founded on human ideas of piety and morality—self-justification's favorites, but which are also the last remaining vestiges of sin.

We are confronted by sectarian groups who deal in ideas about how life ought to be lived, even though such notions are outside the will and purpose of God. They promote views that satisfaction and happiness can be achieved by reverting to the ways of the past because in the fiction of their own minds they remember how life "used to be" better.

One must know God through a living relationship in order to teach about faith. Its meaning must flow like streams of life-giving water out of a believer's heart (John 7:37-38).

The responsibility to properly witness to the Christian faith is part of our call to discipleship. The cost of being a disciple of Christ is to deny oneself. One cannot be a true disciple of Christ unless he gives up everything he has.

To empty our hearts is to make room for Christ. Only then can the Holy Spirit of God rule our minds for bringing to all people the Good News of the Gospel.

Our teaching, therefore, is witnessing to what God has done through Christ. It is not a detailed agenda to regiment people.

Believers teach by witnessing to their living relationship with God. The example of their own lives must proclaim lives in union with Christ. Christian witness is to the glory of God in believers. This must become visible like a beacon if others are to be led to Christ so that they also may see, believe, and become saved.

Only the zealot, whose behavior fringes on fanaticism, wants to see things differently. Because of limited vision, zealous people know no other way but a brute force approach of flesh and muscle for witnessing to the glory of God. These false teachers are so opinionated that they fail to realize that brute force is a technique used to enslave people, whereas the Gospel of Christ is God's message of Good News to set people free in the spirit. The task of preaching and witnessing to the Gospel of Christ is an appeal to the spirit that brings people the truth about God so that all people in the world may become faithful workers on earth on behalf of the Kingdom of God.

We cannot teach faith with an approach of "mind over matter." The power of positive thinking is but another diversion that leads people away from knowing God. Like all other teaching that is not based on the authority of Christ and the inspiration of the Holy Spirit, "positive thinking" also lacks the authority of the Word of God.

Theology by the sword extended its millenium of power into the 20th century. People today are more sophisticated than those involved in the religious wars that lasted for thirty years (1618-1648) and spread blood all over continental Europe. It is truly an irony that people engage in armed conflict to bring the love of God to others as servants of the Gospel.

Despite warnings from Christ (Matthew 7:21-23), people continue dealing in a conceptual approach to religion instead of witnessing to the truth of the Gospel. Substance is not enhanced by any acquired expertise in teaching.

Evil surfaces when indoctrination tactics fail because of falsehood. For example, Martin Luther was branded a heretic and condemned to die because he dared to correct falsehood and stood by God's plan that salvation is by grace through faith. The best that church doctrine can do is produce "a most likely story," whereas Christ's teaching is eternal truth that sets people free (John 8:31-32).

Improvements in attitudes are noticeable in the recent past. The Roman Catholic Second Vatican Council (1962-65) has made room for dialogues. And Christians throughout the world hail religious tolerance because of it. Ecumenism on local levels has become central in witnessing to Christ today. But let us remember that our obligation to God has as its foundation Christ and eternal truth.

Worldly councils can only point to God as the true authority to restore order in human lives. Therefore, Christians must celebrate ecumenism today because the Body of Christ recognizes the need for united fellowship in God's presence and acknowledges the guidance of the Holy Spirit in everyday activities. These objectives must not be confused with the commendable achievements by which people practice religious tolerance.

Observation throughout the ages has revealed human character as quick for action, slow in learning, and arrogant to see the other point of view—even God's will in Christ's teaching. It was as recently as 1984 that theologians from the Roman Catholic Church in the United States openly acknowledged God's plan of salvation by grace through faith. St. Paul's tutorial in Romans 8 is indeed appropriate to help Christians today prepare themselves for making God known to all peoples everywhere.

Despite some progress, the Body of Christ remains polarized. The church has really never suffered from any lack of personal opinions about truth. Nor has there been a shortage of statements. The influential bishops' letters on peace and economics are among the more recent examples. Remnants of earlier attempts to integrate religion and worldly affairs—like the religious activities at the beginning of the industrial revolution during the latter half of the 19th century—are with us still in the classification scheme that labels Protestantism (because of belief in work ethic) as being close to capitalism, whereas Roman Catholicism (because of its constant appeals to share wealth with the poor) is linked to socialism.

And there are other influences. Special interest groups formed by fundamentalists from the Southern Baptist Convention have created a national forum for debating prayers in public schools. The politically active Moral Majority is a

sectarian group that is not at all hesitant to impress upon
the general public its idiosyncracies. Therefore, in all this
worldly confusion Christians must remember their obligation for the glory of God on earth while at the same time
living out God's expectations as a matter of personal commitment. Religious and political freedom is granted to all
citizens by the United States Constitution.

While secular law protects religious freedom, ecclesiastical law is known to control spiritual behavior. For example,
members of the Roman Catholic Church who have remar-
ried without having their previous marriage annulled by
the church—even though such annulments have no legal
status in the secular world—cannot participate in Holy
Communion.

The world today is further overburdened with violence.
Religious fanatics will use the "sword" in its physical sense
to demonstrate "true religion" according to the definition of
their warped thinking. For example, fringe elements of
Islam control the inhabitants of Iran. Lebanon's people
must live in daily fear of terrorism that is sparked by
religious insanity among Muslims and Christians alike. Intolerance in India is subduing masses of people with its
outmoded caste system. The largest democracy in the
world experienced Theology of the Sword in the murder of
its prime minister.

The Western world is not immune to religious intolerance and its manifestation in terrorism. What many people
would prefer to describe as a political struggle in the
fighting among Protestants and Roman Catholics in Northern Ireland is a religious issue. It has become Christianity's
shame.

To make satanic acts palatable for public acceptance,
individuals are quick to invent labels and phrases to justify
these activities. The rest of civilization stands by and

washes its hands from guilt as long as "the other people's problems" are a safe distant away.

Instead of fulfilling our responsibility as disciples of Christ by speaking out against wrongs in the world, people are silently watching—secretly wishing that the party they are rooting for will win.

As these struggles go on, followers of the Theology of the Sword and by the sword gather in sacred assemblies to unify "religion." Conclaves and councils are formed to iron out little differences in philosophy. Experts compromise a little here and there. But they totally neglect to seek guidance from the Holy Spirit for knowing the truth about God, God's will, and the purpose for our lives as the only thing that must matter.

Any false teaching and coercion must be exposed in light of truth as revealed to believers by the Holy Spirit of God. Christ says "when the Spirit of truth comes, he will guide you into all the truth; for he will not speak on his own authority, but whatever he hears he will speak, and he will declare to you the things that are to come. He will glorify me, for he will take what is mine and declare it to you. All that the Father has is mine; therefore I said that he will take what is mine and declare it to you." (John 16:13-15)

One cannot instill hope in people with a weapon of destruction, which either sword or coercion represents.

4. The Horror of War

Through the rejection of God, people deny themselves the opportunity of letting God work His will to accomplish divine purpose. As long as the sin in human nature is allowed to run rampant, people are proud, arrogant, conceited, selfish, and full of empty boasts.

We find this in Biblical history. The prophet Isaiah

quotes the people of Judah as he describes the attitude of the people of Moab: "We have heard of the pride of Moab, how proud he was; of his arrogance, his pride, and his insolence—his boasts are false." (Isaiah 16:6)

Consequently, Jeremiah prophesied that Moab would be humbled: "We have heard of the pride of Moab—he is very proud—of his loftiness, his pride, and his arrogance, and the haughtiness of his heart. I know his insolence, says the LORD; his boasts are false, his deeds are false . . . And I will bring to an end in Moab, says the LORD, him who offers sacrifice in the high place and burns incense to his god." (Jeremiah 48:29-30, 35)

And the Biblical record shows God's judgment on Moab: "On all the housetops of Moab and in the squares there is nothing but lamentation; for I have broken Moab like a vessel for which no one cares, says the LORD. How it is broken! How they wail! How Moab has turned his back in shame! So Moab has become a derision and a horror to all that are round about him." (Jeremiah 48:38-39)

As the judgment is executed, a greater horror is experienced by those forced to witness the atrocities of war: "When the king of Moab saw that the battle was going against him, he took with him seven hundred swordsmen to break through, opposite the king of Edom; but they could not. Then he took his eldest son who was to reign in his stead, and offered him for a burnt offering upon the wall. And there came great wrath upon Israel; and they withdrew from him and returned to their own land." (2 Kings 3:26-27)

Let us briefly examine the history of the Moabites. The Moabites and the Ammonites were the descendants of Lot, born by his daughters, after God had destroyed Sodom and Gomorrah.

Moses refers to the Moabites as he contrasts the nature

of true power and human arrogance: "The LORD is my strength and my song, and he has become my salvation; this is my God, and I will praise him, my father's God, and I will exalt him . . . Thy right hand, O LORD, glorious in power, thy right hand, O LORD, shatters the enemy . . . Thou didst stretch out thy right hand, the earth swallowed them." (Exodus 15:2, 6, 12)

But concerning the strength of the nations, Moses writes: "Now are the chiefs of Edom dismayed; the leaders of Moab, trembling seizes them; all the inhabitants of Canaan have melted away." (Exodus 15:15)

Lot's descendants are part of our Christian heritage. It was in Moabite territory that Moses explained God's laws to the Israelites. And atop Mount Nebo, high above the plains of Moab, God showed Moses the promised land, thereby establishing prophetically the destiny of the Israelites to live secured and in service to God.

But the record also shows the external influence on the faithfulness of the chosen people of God. For despite God's obvious presence for guidance and protection (Exodus 23:20-21), Balaam succeeded in making Israel turn away from God.

Because the Israelites disobeyed God, the king of Moab conquered them—not with might or sorcery, but with gifts of pleasure. Through them the Israelites became unfaithful to God: "While Israel dwelt in Shittim the people began to play the harlot with the daughters of Moab. These invited the people to the sacrifices of their gods, and the people ate, and bowed down to their gods. So Israel yoked himself to Baal of Peor. And the anger of the LORD was kindled against Israel." (Numbers 25:1-3)

War, with its many byproducts of horror, is the fruit of faithlessness and disobedience.

Whenever the sin in human nature tries to satisfy greed,

man strikes out to get by force what others have received as a blessing from God. Any subsequent war, and its accompanying terror, inflicts horrors more deadly than the most potent poison on earth. Fear claims victory over body and soul.

Because scar tissues of war are a constant reminder of humanity's failure to get along with one another, future generations are forced to live in continuous threats of life. Even peaceful people will be pressured to respond to tools of an aggressor nation with an even greater appropriation of resources for their own defense to maintain peace. Satan desires people to live in fear. Fear is among the sly serpent's methods by which he tries to keep us away from the presence of God.

Additional trauma increases the fear about wars even further. Technological advances in warfare have raised the level of destructive power to the potential of total annihilation. Wipeouts of entire civilizations are highly probable.

Fears about war, therefore, are not wild imaginations. They are real threats to spiritual well-being in all situations, where the love of God does not control people's destiny.

Even faithful believers feel the pressure of horrors. The moment of truth demands that we demonstrate trust in God. Because faithfulness alone secures spiritual rest amidst all the turmoil in the world, obedience to the will of God separates Christ's followers.

We live according to God's promise. And we hold firm to the hope that God will look after us and provide for our safety. Christ, indeed, has promised to be with us "always, to the close of the age." (Matthew 28:20)

This hope is part of God's universal truth in the Gospel. There is no power on earth that can separate believers from the love of God through Christ Jesus. Additionally, since our life is in God's service, we are sustained by the power of God's Holy Spirit for witnessing to God's grace in and around us.

St. Paul describes the grace of God in his letter to the Church at Rome as the steadfastness of God's love. In a way that reaffirms his own belief in the love of God, St. Paul poses the question: "If God is for us, who is against us?" (Romans 8:31b)

And St. Paul continues: "Who shall separate us from the love of Christ? Shall tribulation, or distress, or persecution, or famine, or nakedness, or peril, or sword? . . . No, in all these things we are more than conquerors through him who loved us." (Romans 8:35,37)

With these words, St. Paul is refreshing the memory of believers with the teaching of Christ that restored fellowship with God is the way of obedience to Christ's leadership, whose obedience to God secured a relationship for believers that is best summarized in a shepherd's concern for his flock: "I am the good shepherd; I know my own and my own know me, as the Father knows me and I know the Father; and I lay down my life for the sheep." (John 10:14-15)

Therefore, the answer to the question, "Where is God?" is hidden in faith and trust in God. Faithfulness and obedience to God are the visible signs of Christ's followers.

The faithful believer in Christ knows the presence of God! In the noise of violent conflict, God calms the soul so that we can truly appreciate the serenity of God's presence.

We have peace, because we believe in God's promise. Our faithfulness is the key to God's assurance of peace. The Book of Revelations has recorded the foretaste of Christ's promise. This visionary text addresses the Church in Smyrna: "Be faithful unto death, and I will give you the crown of life." (Revelation 2:10b)

But why does God tolerate war?

God does not tolerate war!

God does not incite war. People do!

War is a desire of human nature. Speaking on behalf of God, Moses told the Israelites as they journeyed to the promised land: "I call heaven and earth to witness against you this day, that I have set before you life and death, blessing and curse; therefore choose life, that you and your descendants may live, loving the LORD your God, obeying his voice, and cleaving to him; for that means life to you and length of days. . . ." (Deuteronomy 30:19-20)

As a guide for all believers, God's challenge is summarized by Christ in the two Great Commandments (Matthew 22:37-39). The viewpoint is different. But the message is the same.

So, let us not act surprised that the burden of responsibilities for making war rests with people.

The only surprise that should make us shudder is the irony that turns out to be the real horror of all times: Warring nations pray to the same God for victory.

Despite this being so, we must not become disheartened because of confusion. Neither should we let ourselves be fooled. What may appear as sincere prayers to God for deliverance, are many times just instant ramblings of pious words.

The evil in human nature tries to justify its rebellion toward God through its own system of piety. The difference between the true disciples of Christ and those that consider themselves followers is catastrophic. One can usually notice this difference in the lifestyle of people. It commonly shows up as a distinguishable contrast of life and death: salvation in God's presence or condemnation to hell (Luke 13:22-30).

It is clear that only the true disciples of Christ will search for the will of God when praying for deliverance. Dedicated followers express their trust in God to safely carry them through hardships and horrors, similar to the protection envisioned by the Psalmist when he declared God as the protector of all faithful people: "A thousand may fall at your side, ten thousand at your right hand; but it will not come near you. You will only look with your eyes and see the recompense of the wicked." (Psalms 91:7-8)

Sometimes, horrors can be so overwhelming that many people will lose faith because of them. When this happens, let us not blame such incidents on a righteous and faithful God whose promise of salvation is secured in steadfastness.

It is certain that God will help faithful believers during moments of death and destruction when faith is put to the test, like that of Job was. Such trials establish the worthiness of our spiritual being, for in the flesh we are made to realize the futility of our human nature. Our spirit alone can be renewed with strength from God.

Horrors of war are threatening to people in the world when they lose faith and put their own ambitions ahead of a firm commitment of faithfulness to God. Therefore, let us always remember that God had created the human race to be faithful.

Let there not be any doubt, some fears have substance. Man has advanced to the frightful state of existence where "bigger is better" borders on insanity. By relying totally on human intelligence, limited as it is, we have constructed weapons of mass destruction without really having a true understanding of how to harness their power, take care of their effect on anything living, or even dispose of them responsibly when not wanted or needed.

We seem to be more concerned about the immediacy of economic gain in weapon development than any ultimate effects on people or nature. If all these resources of God that are being wasted on tools of destruction were to be used to the glory of God, the way God had intended them to be used, then peace would be the assurance by divine decree.

As long as mankind concentrates resources, energies, and talents on weapons of destruction, then these very same weapons in which people place their security become a horror to future generations. And the threat of annihilation is indeed real.

The threat is real, because we have created not knowing what we are actually doing, despite the fact that well-educated experts claim to be in control. This will always be the case whenever people shut God out of their lives.

A great many fears nurture on past wounds. Hurt and resentment burden the souls of people because the scar tissue from past conflicts has inadequately healed. There are constant reminders of people killed, bodies maimed, and property destroyed through families who suffered the consequences of folly in leadership.

The Shepherd-King David, despite his shortcomings of human nature, had as his most outstanding feature a deep faith and devotion to God. David knew how to rule because of his intimate relationship with God. But he also knew how to accept the punishment that God sent because of his shortcomings.

The scars of any past wounds of war can only be healed by God when a faith-trust-love relationship is the basis for life. Total dependence on God is the only way that will prevent future wounds from being inflicted. And our reliance on God will further quench any fear. Threats that otherwise might overpower the new existence in the Spirit will then have no power over believers.

Thus we profess Christ. As Christians we claim peace through promise. The truth of the Word of God is authority and promise.

The authority is clearly defined: "All authority in heaven and on earth has been given to me." Matthew 28:18)

And the promise is precisely given: "I am with you always, to the close of the age." (Matthew 28:20)

19

The Peace of God

The Peace of God is the secure knowledge that our life is not wasted and useless but a fulfillment of the will and purpose of God. In our total submission to the Holy Spirit, we know God as Creator and share a mutual love-relationship, through our life in union with Christ, our Redeemer.

The Peace of God gives us light. It guides us on the path of God's righteousness. This light helps us envision with the eyes of our soul the work of God that must be done by us.

The Peace of God brings us truth. The teaching of Christ is a daily renewal of wonders as the Holy Spirit constantly reveals to believers the truth about God.

The Peace of God is life. In the security of God's presence believers see the turmoil of a violent existence on earth put to rest. As Jesus Christ commanded the wind, "Be quiet!" and he said to the waves, "Be still!" so Christ leads believers through difficulties in the world by telling us: "Let not your hearts be troubled; believe in God, believe also in me. In my Father's house are many rooms; if it were not so, would I have told you that I go to prepare a place for you? And when I go and prepare a place for you, I will come again and will take you to myself, that where I am you may be also." (John 14:1-3)

As a shepherd leads his flock to pasture, and the sheep

175

willingly follow—not really knowing where they are going—so Christ our Shepherd leads us to secure the nourishment for eternal life.

Life on earth is a pilgrimage of short duration. But when all is said and done, we are assured of rest. This rest is the fulfillment of divine promise that assures our return to God.

The Peace of God protects us from trials and temptations, like an umbrella that provides shade from the burning sun. It shields us securely in preparation for the end of our days when we will be invited to the eternal feast.

The Peace of God is hope. In his most depressed existence, Solomon contemplated the uselessness of his earthly life, as he came to realize how selfishly he had consumed his great wealth. He enjoyed the pleasures of the world so much that he missed being faithful and obedient to God. The departing thoughts of the Philosopher's wisdom is a summary of fact describing earthly life: "After all this, there is only one thing to say: Have reverence for God, and obey his commands, because this is all that man was created for. God is going to judge everything we do, whether good or bad, even things done in secret." (Ecclesiastes 12:13-14)TEV

Light—Truth—Life. These are the combined attributes of the Peace of God that Christ has secured for us with His death on the Cross. Let us walk in this peace and rest our problems in the Gospel of Christ as the divine gift of God's righteousness.

When we live in the Peace of God, then we are also at peace within ourselves. And the prayers of our most inner selves will echo praises and admirations of God: "Hallowed be Thy name. Thy Kingdom come; thy will be done, on earth as it is in heaven."

As we live in the Peace of God and through it know

security, then we have a duty to share it. St. Paul's departing words of assurance and blessings to the Church at Philippi are appropriate for making known the only peace of value in the world: "And the peace of God, which passes all understanding, will keep your hearts and your minds in Christ Jesus." (Philippians 4:7)

So be it!

Index to Scripture Passages

Subject Index